How to Get Through

Hell on Earth

Without Drinking a Keg
or Kicking a Garden Gnome

Real-Life Stories + Lessons

By Ryn Gargulinski

RYNSKI LIFE

Rynski Life Publications
Copyright © 2023 Ryn Gargulinski
All rights reserved.
ISBN: 978-1-937539-09-2

Dedication

This book is dedicated to the Cosmos.
They know why:)

Acknowledgements

Perhaps if I were fully enlightened I would thank everybody in my life, even those who contributed to awful experiences, since they helped me become who I am today.

Heck with that. Let's just say I must be about three-quarters enlightened.

A big round of thanks goes to editor man John Saxtan for his patience, professionalism and amazingly keen eye.

Mom and Dad get thanks for never giving up on me. My brother gets added for putting up with me.

A big thanks to Beezel for his ongoing love, pep talks and knowing just when I could use a pizza.

Soul sister Shelley, you keep me going!

Several rounds of thanks go to all the incredible people I've met in recovery throughout my journey, along with all the friends I've made, the amazing bosses, professors and teachers I've had, and the many magical people I've connected with.

Just because they don't all get mentioned in this book doesn't mean I don't love them. I love them greatly and thank them heartily from the very happy bottom of my heart.

Disclaimer

Names have been changed.
Places and stories have not.

Table of Contents

Introduction	1
Part 1: The Downfall	3
Part 2: Sea Legs	103
Part 3: Beyond My Wildest Dreams	145
Part 4: Making Magic in Your Own Life	275
Books + Resources	291
About the Author	293

Introduction

For the record, I never kicked a garden gnome (although I have punched out an inflatable snowman). But I have also consumed my share of kegs over the years. In fact, one of the ways I stay sober today is by reminding myself I used up my whole life's alcohol allotment by the time I hit 29.

My alcoholic bottom was easily the most intense hell on earth I've ever experienced. But it certainly hasn't been the only one. I've been stalked, homeless, jobless, friendless, and suffocated under the weight of depression. I've been broken on the rack with grief, eaten to the bone by fear.

But I'm still here, still alive – and happier than ever. That's because I didn't give up. I didn't lie down and die. I instead found a way of living that helped me get through the litany of hells I've experienced – so I can share my experiences with you.

Fasten your seatbelt. You're coming on a journey peppered with a host of hells, along with info on ways I got through them. Many solutions are woven into the stories, and some early solutions ended up being later roadblocks that I needed to get rid of to soar.

The last chapter delivers a quick overview of strategies I continue to use to get through any new hells that come my way. And as long as we're alive, it's likely they'll keep coming. That's just the way life goes.

No matter how, where, when, or how long we live, we're all going to face our own varieties of hell on earth. While we may not be able to control some of the stuff that's thrown our way, we can consciously decide what we do with it.

We can let it drag us down, wailing about being a victim as we rot in the gutter. Or we can use it to build us up into an unstoppable force that has the power of love, God and two big dogs on our side.

I went with the latter. It's infinitely more fun. It's also infinitely more interesting to look at life on earth as a big adventure.

We're here to fully experience both its beauty and its horror – and hopefully enjoy the ride.

Ryn Gargulinski [Rynski]

Cape Coral, Florida
January 26, 2023

Part 1
The Downfall

To live with.
To live without.
Who gives a shit.
Guinness Stout.

-Ryn Gargulinski, 1988

Now What?

If you're not sure how to start a story, I was told to start it with a dead body. In this case, the dead body just so happened to be mine.

I wasn't physically dead, of course, or I wouldn't be writing this. But I was pretty much dead on the inside – not to mention in a hell of a lot of pain.

My head was pounding. My throat was raw and burning. My mouth tasted like the inside of an old shoe. But the greatest pain was in my nose. Something was making it ache from the inside out, as if a Matchbox truck had been stuffed inside it.

Something was wrong. Very wrong. So wrong I was scared to open my eyes. If I just laid there a little longer, maybe it would all go away. Maybe I'd wake up again, this time without the pain in my nose, the pounding in my head, and the fear swirling in my gut like a tilt-a-whirl.

My nose was about to burst. I instinctively tried to reach for it, to pull out whatever was making it hurt, only to realize I couldn't move my arm. Or my other arm.

What have I done now?

That's when I opened my eyes. Both of my wrists were tethered to a hospital bed with leather buckle cuffs, the kind they use in old haunted asylums.

Great. Chained to the bed. A toy truck stuffed up my nose. I wondered if my head was turned around backwards, too.

I heard a murmuring voice: "She's awake."

Then another: "You're one lucky girl. You should have been dead."

Dead? Dead from what?

A very brief piece of the night before started filtering back to me. A group of about five of us teens, hanging out before the homecoming football game. Two brand new bottles of booze. One of them gin.

Them handing me the bottle of gin. Me wanting to show them how cool I was, slamming the whole thing in about 52 seconds.

Someone saying, "Holy shit."

Then blackness. More blackness. Nothing.

Then this. Waking up tethered to a hospital bed, tubes shoved up my nose so they could pump my stomach.

Death from alcohol poisoning generally comes from a blood alcohol level of 0.5%. Mine had been .46%.

Ooops.

I was tethered to the bed because I had been brought in to the hospital totally out of control. Kicking and screaming and cussing and punching. I may have even tried to bite someone.

It was never confirmed if my head spun all the way around, but I would not have been surprised if it had.

Everything hurt that much. But the physical pain was nothing compared to the fear and shame. Shame over doing something dumb, once again. Something I couldn't even remember but had a bad, bad feeling about.

Fear someone may have seen some of what happened. Fear of what kind of punishment my parents would have in store.

And although the death wasn't necessarily to my earthly being at that point, the situation had been a death for several things.

The death of pretending to fit in. The death of caring about much of anything. The death of hope.

I had crossed that line that had been beckoning me for years. Crossed the line into full-blown alcoholism.

I was a freshman in high school. I was 14 years old.

Waking up with tubes up my nose on Saturday was a walk in the park compared to what happened next.

That's because I showed up to school that next Monday as if nothing had happened. The moment I walked into that brightly lit hallway and everyone went dead silent and stared, I knew my worst fears had come true.

They knew what happened. All the kids in the school knew what happened. Heck, they knew what happened better than I did, since I still knew nothing.

I just knew it was bad. My face burned as I tried to walk nonchalantly to my orange locker, hoping no one would notice my entire head was burning bright red in embarrassment and dread.

Everyone's head turned to follow me, like I had six heads, 22 eyeballs and a forked tail.

Throughout my childhood, I had gotten used to people staring at me, making fun of me. The birthmark on my face. The missing front tooth I accidentally knocked out during a fall at age 2. The last name Gargulinski.

But this was nothing like those elementary school barbs. These eyes were sending evil darts that went right through me.

I was a specimen being dissected, like those worms or frogs on the black waxy platforms in science class. I could almost smell the formaldehyde oozing out of my pores.

I wanted to die.

I got my books, went to my class. Heard the loudspeaker blaring my name about two minutes into the session.

"Gargulinski, come to the principal's office immediately. Gargulinski."

I wanted to die double.

I slithered out of my seat. Willed myself to shrink or altogether disappear as I made way out of the classroom and into the hall. All those staring, gaping faces were still following my every move. The formaldehyde stench got stronger.

"Why are you in school?" was the first thing the principal asked me when I sat down in his office.

Because it's Monday? Because Mom would yell if I didn't go?

Ends up I had been suspended, something they told me on Friday during the blackout.

Oh.

Now I wasn't sure which was worse. Being in school and facing those silent, staring faces – or going home to face the unbearable disappointment in my parents' faces that was surely waiting there.

Bits and dribbles of what supposedly happened that fateful homecoming Friday inevitably made their way to my ears. I heard I screamed profanities at the cops who were called to calm down some out-of-control drunk teen. Others said I puked on the principal.

I noticed no remnants of vomit on his suit when he sent me home that Monday.

I never tried to verify any of it. Nor do I want to. All I know for sure was that I felt like a total idiot and that I had been suspended. That, and I could probably expect four years of suburban Michigan high school hell from my trashed reputation.

Oh, and one more thing. That my near-death drinking experience that would most likely mark the end of any logical person's drinking career, was merely the big debut of mine.

High school dragged on like a carcass behind a truck. Every day brought another layer of hurt and shame. Instead of showing my pain or telling anyone how awful it was to be a modern-day pariah, I pretended it didn't matter.

I'll put up a wall and hate you first, since you'll end up hating me anyway. I hate you first, so there. I'll just act weirder and stranger and wear way too much eyeliner as I pretend this is the way I want it all to be. So there. So there. So there!

No matter how much pain I had to endure throughout the school day, alcohol would take it away at night. Or at least on the nights I could get it.

Nobody was going to sell to a minor in Troy, Michigan. But if I drove REALLY fast to downtown Detroit before my job near the mall, I could buy booze to hide in the trunk and then smuggle into my bedroom or the nearby woods.

Beer was my drink of choice. I already saw how hard liquor could kill you from a single bottle. Figured beer was safer. It was also cheaper. But sometimes I'd have to leave it in the trunk for a while before I could smuggle it in the house.

One time that didn't work out too well for Budweiser cans in the winter. By the time I could sneak them in the house to drink them, they were frozen solid.

I thought putting them in the oven would be a good idea to thaw them out.

It took me a few minutes to realize the hissing and popping sounds coming from the kitchen were my Budweiser cans exploding in the oven.

On weekends when I didn't have the car to go to work, I'd walk five miles to the bus stop that would take me to downtown Detroit.

This let me drink as much as I wanted without worrying about driving. I could also hang out in my favorite haunts, which were abandoned houses that were now used as drug dens.

While I never saw another person in my favorite dilapidated house, I did see abandoned needles. And a flattened dead cat.

As I leaned against the falling-off kitchen sink, swilling my Budweiser and staring at ripped-up wallpaper, a bright idea occurred to me. Wouldn't it be funny to take that cat to school and put it in the trophy cabinet?

The more I drank, the better the idea became. But I didn't want to actually touch the cat. He no longer smelled. He was mummified. But still.

I found a garbage bag and a piece of rope. I put the garbage bag around the cat and wrapped the rope around its neck. The cat was completely hidden in the bag, which I dragged behind me to the bus stop.

Once back in suburbia, I hid the cat in the woods until the next morning. Then dragged it the one mile to school. Snuck out to the main school lobby when no one was looking, placed the cat front and center in the main trophy cabinet.

You peg me as an outcast; I'll show you an outcast. I'll be the best damn outcast on the planet!

Later that day, I heard a high-pitched scream coming from the front lobby area. I went over to look, saw a couple of girls crying. The trophy cabinet door was open. A janitor was putting something in a bag.

"What's in the bag?" I asked with my most innocent face. For the record, it's tough to look innocent when half your head's shaved, you're wearing dark black eyeshadow, and you have a padlock as choker around your neck.

He looked at me answered with a scowl. "You know damn well what's in the bag."

The trophy cabinet was never left unlocked again.

The cat in the trophy cabinet was one of my few triumphs in high school, a time peppered with many losses.

OK fine, winning journalism awards for my work with the high school newspaper I guess would count as triumphs – although I felt more horrified than proud when they put my name on the big sign outside the school, the one you could see from the main road.

Instead of seeing "First Place Journalism Award" on the sign, I saw "Weird Chick that Everyone Hates." Or at least everyone hated but Annette.

Annette was truly an angel. She not only remained my friend when everyone else shunned me like a leper, but also turned me on to Led Zeppelin.

Gotta be some divine intervention in that. Or I thought so until I did my psychology report on the rumors of the band's devil worship. I was particularly fascinated by the rumor that you could play "Stairway to Heaven" backwards on the record player and hear a secret message to the devil.

After nearly wrecking the entire Zeppelin IV album to listen for the message, I heard it. I did. And it made my skin crawl. As dark and dreary as I pretended to be, there's no way I wanted to play around with Satan.

But I definitely had to include that scary backwards message in my psychology report.

Like any good high school student that doesn't care if she lives or dies, I had waited until the night before to sit down and actually type up the report. Started printing it out around 2 a.m.

And as soon as the page containing the backwards message came to print, the printer jammed. The red lights flashed. The paper went spewing wildly from the machine.

No way. NO WAY! It's possessed. The printer is possessed!

I screeched, wailed, cried. Shouted and pounded my fists. Shook the printer.

How the heck am I supposed to get this done in time?! The printer, the printer is possessed!!!

For some reason, my mom woke up and came downstairs.

Her mother, Grandma P, was the one who told me how to trick the devil if he ever came calling. Just ask him to bring you water in a sieve.

Water in a sieve, water in sieve. You can trick the devil by asking him to bring you water in sieve.

I guess I had forgotten to ask that in my panic. But evidently Mom remembered some kind of something. She got the printer to work properly, promising me it was not possessed. No matter. I would never use that brand of printer again.

High school stunk. Living in suburban Michigan stunk. Having the devil living in the printer stunk. If I could just get out of there, things would be better.

Since my mom was a proud graduate of the University of Michigan, I applied to Michigan State. I think most of the things I did back then were simply done to piss people off.

I was accepted to Michigan State, a bummer since I didn't want to go there. That's where a big chunk of the suburban high school students were going.

Why on earth would I want a total replay of this hell, but on a bigger campus in East Lansing?

Besides, I had the distinct feeling if I stuck around suburban Michigan I would turn into a bored housewife whose highlight in life was sneaking drinks in the laundry room on wash day. I'd probably get a big belly and droopy boobs and end up consistently passing out on other people's lawns.

I needed something bigger and better.

I needed a place where my weirdness would blend in, not stick out like a weed on a field full of daffodils. Or more like a meteor crater in a field of daffodils.

I needed a slimy, grimy, gritty city, not a picket-fence suburbia where everyone had 2.4 kids and double-car garage. I needed a place where the outer filth and chaos matched my inner feelings of chaos and absolute despair.

I needed to go live on the streets of New York City.

When the idea of moving to New York was first hatched, I didn't honestly think I'd end up on the streets. I thought I'd be merrily living with a group of other runaway teens in an abandoned building headed by a man named Lan (or Lon).

That's what my friend Dobie had told me. Yes, I managed to get another friend, in addition to Annette. Actually, I had a few pals by the end of my high school stint. And I secretly thanked every one of them for giving me a second chance, even though I vehemently pretended that's the last thing I wanted from anyone.

Dobie had a makeshift mohawk and a box of half-eaten moldy cheese pizza under his bed.

I had assumed – or at least hoped – the first half was eaten before it got moldy.

I found the pizza by accident when I extended my leg and it got caught on something beneath his bed. We were sitting on the floor in his bedroom, discussing our big New York plan.

Dobie had heard of this Lan or Lon guy through whatever channels, and he was sick of suburbia, too. We'd find this Lan-Lon man in a squat near Thompkins Square Park. He'd let all the runaway kids live there for free as long as they helped him fix up the building.

No parents. Free rent. I immediately envisioned joyfully hauling a bucket of paint onto a stoop, painting the outside of the building a bright white with all kinds of Ryn art on it for a whimsical yet creepy touch.

How cool is that? I'm in.

Dobie and I planned to take a Greyhound to New York together, on whatever date sometime in July or August after high school graduation. Mom had begged me enough to please stay in school long enough to graduate.

OK fine. While I did finish the prison sentence called high school, I was unable to honor that faraway July or August departure date Dobie had in mind. That's because I started a fight with Mom for whatever reason one day in June – and I had to get out, NOW, THIS INSTANT!

I created a Plan B on the spot.

I cashed the check from my gas station job, where I probably owed them more than my check for all the Doritos and Mountain Dew I consumed during my shifts. I also grabbed the $100 bill I knew Mom hid in a picture frame on her dresser. Snagged the gallon jug of white wine from my parents' fridge.

Packed my body-sized duffel bag with all the things I would need to survive in New York: my markers, my cassette tapes and Walkman, my sketchbooks.

Dobie drove me to the Greyhound station. Away I went. He was going to join me later, after I had established our position in the Ryn-art building with the Lan-Lon man.

Goodbye. See you soon. Good riddance mean-ole Michigan. I'm going to a better place.

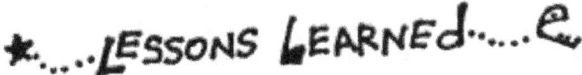
*.....LESSONS LEARNEd......e

Living in hate is exhausting.

Running from life is exhausting.

Don't drink gin.

New York City – 1988

Like a wet-hot rag, the acrid stench of urine hit me in the face the minute I stepped off the Greyhound bus. It was hot. It was muggy. It was noisy enough to make my teeth rattle.

Welcome to New York City.

The stench was coming from a corner of the Port Authority bus terminal, a large, echoing chamber full of shuffling drug dealers and zipping businessmen.

I started asking if any of them heard of Lon or Lan who lived in an abandoned building near Tompkins Square Park.

"Tompkins what?" asked one businessman as he hurried away on his rat race to nowhere.

"Smoke?" asked a drug dealer, one of the many whispering a little mantra of "smoke, sense, smoke sense, smoke, smoke, sense, sense."

"No," I told him. I didn't want to buy any pot. But I would like some acid.

"I know a guy," he told me. Just give him the money, and he'll go hook up with the guy. Be right back.

"Yeah, right."

"Here," he insisted, "Hold my hat so you know I'll come back."

I gave him a $20 bill. He gave me his filthy, beat-up red baseball cap.

About 30 minutes later, I was still holding the cap. The man who knew a man with LSD was absolutely nowhere to be found.

New York has a steep and fast learning curve.

I just got an F on my first exam.

I ranked about a C- on my next venture, which was getting from the midtown Manhattan bus station to this place called Tompkins Square Park.

High marks came from walking in the right direction for some reason. But I got points off for the heavy load.

New York was going through a sweltering heat wave. Not only was I lugging a body-bag-sized duffel packed with markers and cassette tapes, but I was burdened with my heavy-as-hell, faux-fur lined leather jacket. Oh yeah. And I was wearing my combat boots.

Can't go running off to NYC without a leather jacket and combat boots.

I spotted a convenience store with a beer sign in the window. Sounded like the perfect idea. But then again, a beer had always sounded like the perfect idea.

I looked around for someone who at least looked like they were over the age of 21 to buy a beer for me. Michigan drinking age was 21. I was 18.

The only places in Michigan that would sell to anyone under 21 were the seedy liquor stores in the bowels of Detroit, the ones with bullet-proof Plexiglas protecting the cashier. I knew them well.

No one was really lingering around. And anyone I tried to make eye contact with immediately averted their gaze. That was new to me at the time, a New York habit I would quickly learn to adopt.

Hell with it. I went in the store, snagged a Heineken from the fridge, and put it on the counter. I made sure to stand up taller so I looked older as I waited for the man at the register to take the beer away and tell me to shoo. Had happened all the time in Michigan.

But he instead nonchalantly rang it up and asked for $1.25.

Wha??!! A massive surge of excitement bubbled in my stomach. When I went to hand him exact change, the butterflies whooshed up my body, nearly blowing the top of my head off.

This was even better than finding hidden Christmas presents under my parents' bed in April.

I then saw the sign by the register that proclaimed New York's legal drinking age was 18.

Yes. Yes. Yes. YESSSSS! I was awestruck. I was elated. I was over the moon. I was home.

Additional confirmation that New York was the place to be came when I finally arrived at Tompkins Square Park. The midtown area surrounding the bus station was all ho-hum boring really tall office buildings.

The landscape remained kind of the same along the 50-plus block walk I had taken south. Even if the buildings weren't all offices, they housed apartments or storefronts I had no interest in visiting (unless there was a beer sign in the window).

Once I got below East 14th Street, the whole vibe started to change. Raggedy looking people with raggedy paper coffee cups were dappled here and there.

Storefronts looked shabbier. People did the same. No more whizzing Mr. Businessmen in three-piece suits. Now we had raggedy baggedy people with scruffy shoes and shopping carts. Now this I could relate to.

I kept going and going until I saw the park, packed with what looked like a giant flea market. Little tents and slouchy cardboard boxes were peppered throughout all the grassy areas.

Music was playing. Even plugging my nose couldn't stop the smell of pot from wafting in.

Pot was not my friend. Every time I smoked it, I ended up thinking people were hiding in the bushes, recording my thoughts.

But this fun-and-games scene was no flea market at all. I figured that out went I went up to one of the tents to see what they were selling and a scowling face peered back at me. It was missing teeth.

Oh. The tents weren't for selling. They were for living. People were living in them. And in the boxes, too.

Holy moly this is sooooo wild. I better go get another beer to honor this quite interesting discovery.

Quite by accident, June 1988 had been exactly the right time to run away to Tompkins Square Park. The city was in a homeless crisis, and it looked like the bulk of them lived right here. I would blend in just fine.

Having my weirdness blend in was just one of the perks I figured I'd enjoy while struggling in New York City. I always thought that a lot of my emotional turmoil and stupid problems were brought on by having too much time to think.

The more you think, the more mayhem you can create in your head. If, on the other hand, I were too busy wondering how I was going to eat or where I was going to sleep, I'd have no time to create the chaos.

Pretty clever, right? It was already working. My only thought at the moment was to find Lon-Lan. No time at all to create additional BS. Oh yes, this was a breakthrough. And double yes, I'd need another beer to celebrate.

I quickly learned several things, growing my survival skills by the minute. The giant 32-ounce bottle of Midnight Dragon malt liquor cost less and lasted longer than the tiny 12-ounce Heineken. Had to conserve the $200 I came with, after all. I had already blown $20 on my failed attempt at getting LSD from the man with the beat-up red baseball cap.

I also learned the Tompkins Square Park people living in the tents and cardboard boxes weren't all that friendly. The people with shopping carts were even more ferocious. Don't you dare go near their stuff, even if it's only to ask a question.

And absolutely none of them, or anyone else I came across, had heard of a guy named Lon or Lan. But they do know where a bunch of abandoned buildings are. Right next to the park, in fact. Boarded up, wrapped with police tape, spray-painted or plastered with signs that said things like "Warning," "Do not enter," and "Condemned."

I spent my first New York City night in one of them.

.....LESSONS LEARNEd.....

Don't try to buy drugs at Port Authority.

Keep your head up, your eyes forward and your bag as close to your body as possible.

If you look like you know where you're going, people tend to leave you alone.

One Man and a Puppy

I met Sheldon while crunched inside a Tompkins Square Park gazebo in the rain. There were a handful of bodies in there, all trying to stay as dry as we could during a late-night downpour.

Not everyone who lived in the park had their very own tent, thank you very much.

Several Rastas were smushed in the gazebo, like a rush-hour, pot-smoked sardine can. One by one I went through the batch, asking the two questions I had begun asking everyone.

"Do you know a guy named Lon or Lan?"

"No."

"Oh. OK. Do you know where I could get some acid?"

Sheldon actually said yes! Not to knowing Lan, but being able to get some acid. When the rain stopped pouring, he took off. Then he came back, grinning, and told me to follow him home.

Yes, I was skeptical. I may have been angry, rebellious and messed-up enough to run away to New York, but I wasn't a total idiot. I was skeptical that he'd actually have the drugs, not necessarily skeptical that I'd actually come out of his place alive.

I figured he was scrawny enough that I could probably fight him off if tried to kill me. And I could definitely use a comfy place to relax after a day of sweltering in the sun and an evening getting drenched by a summer rain.

I followed him out of the park, around a pitch-black corner, down a stretch of beat-up street, back through a vacant lot littered with things that may or may not have been people at one point in time.

We arrived at a basement window of one of those buildings with the big "Condemned" thing painted on the front.

The glass was missing. The window was a little bigger than a shoebox. Maybe a boot box. Sheldon slipped through the opening like a seasoned cat. He told me to follow, beckoning with his flashlight. Warned me not to look around the basement as I walked through it.

"You don't want to stir up the junkies."

Evidently these junkies were hidden behind the filthy mattresses propped against the bare brick walls. If you made eye contact, he said, they would come at you.

I wasn't sure if they would come at me asking for money, drugs, a tuna fish sandwich – or if maybe they'd have a jagged needle in their hand, poised to plunge it into my eyeball.

I didn't want to find out.

After I slid into the basement, I stared straight ahead. That now-familiar acrid smell of urine hung in the air like a sour sheet. It mingled with that musty smell that comes from old books at garage sales. I recognized that odor from hanging out and drinking in the abandoned buildings in Detroit.

How nice some smells remained recognizable, even across state lines.

Once through the basement, we were in the main foyer of big, gutted apartment building. Old wooden beams showed through the ramshackle floorboards.

If you looked up on one side of the building, you could see up forever. Or at least to the top of the building, a good six or seven stories up. The floors on that side of the building had all collapsed, leaving a gaping open space.

One the other side of the building, the floors were still in place. It reminded me of a doll house, where you can see all the floors on different levels while moving the little people around to watch TV or sit on the couch.

But there were no TVs or couches. No light except for Sheldon's flashlight. And no staircase either. Just a rickety wooden ladder that no one in their right mind would even attempt to climb.

I went up first. Sheldon following behind with his flashlight. We climbed up to the third floor, where Sheldon had built a kind of fortress.

He first had to open the padlock that was securing one side of a massive sheet of metal to a doorframe. The padlock was secured to a chain looped through a hole in the metal, kind of like a makeshift doorknob.

The other side of the big metal sheet had a few holes down its side, with chain snaked through the metal holes and attached to the other side of the doorframe. There were enough small openings in the wall on either side of doorframe to weave the chain in, out and around the frame.

Guess it was the Alphabet City version of Fort Knox. Instead of having piles of gold behind the door, Sheldon had a pretty cool pad laid out. With furniture, even. I honestly don't remember if he had any lights in the place, although squatters were pretty good at tapping into street lamps and running extension cords into their dwellings.

Not all the windows were boarded up, so enough light came in to have a good look around the place. I also remember a German Shepherd puppy. This was before I was a dog person, but I thought the puppy was cute anyway. Until he kept stealing my cards off the floor when I tried to play solitaire.

Alphabet City was the darling little name for the East Village neighborhood that housed Tompkins Square Park. It got its name from the four main avenues that ran through it: Avenue A, Avenue B, Avenue C and Avenue D.

Sheldon filled me in on all of it as we dropped the promised acid.

Avenue D was closest to the East River, the body of water best known as a dumping ground for sewage pipe waste and murder victims. Wow. I was near the real-life place that likely spawned the term "sleeping with the fishes." Cool.

The closer to Avenue D you got, the more you were putting your life in your hands.

Sheldon's squat was on Avenue C. East 13th Street and Avenue C, to be exact. It was the biggest neighborhood hive of abandoned buildings filled with squatters. Heck, you'd be as hard-pressed to find space here as you would looking for a regular apartment.

And the rents in squats were decidedly cheaper. True, you didn't get electricity or running water. Unless you counted the rain that would inevitably seep through the ceiling during a thunderstorm.

Police had pretty much given up trying to roust people out of the buildings. It was a good idea to get to know your squatting next-door neighbors, so you could either watch out for each other or know who to blame when something went missing.

Hmmm. Maybe I don't need this Lan-Lon guy after all. Maybe I can just claim my own little living space, put a big sheet of metal in front of the front door like Sheldon did.

He must have seen the wheels in my brain churning.

"You can't just go live in a squat that you find," Sheldon warned me. That's also putting your life in your hands. There was a whole hierarchy of sorts and you needed permission from someone, somewhere to even walk into one of the things without asking for trouble.

Sheldon had been living in his fortress for some time, as had several others. Apparently you needed connections if you ever wanted to get in on one of these coveted places. I guess I'd better be nice to Sheldon.

But oh, no – not THAT nice.

Once the acid started kicking in, Sheldon reclined on his bed. It was an actual mattress-bed with actual blankets and pillows. I'm telling you, his squat was outfitted like a regular apartment.

I'm also telling you the idea of even kissing Sheldon was less appealing than the idea of sticking a wire hanger in my eye. But I could tell that's the direction he was aiming for. He was lying on his back on the bed, giving me a look I knew all too well.

The look involved raised eyebrows and typically came after a guy would buy me beer, hand me a joint or otherwise do something for me. Now it was time to do something for them, right?

Wrong. So wrong. I had a trick that usually worked to get me out of it. I just played dumb.

Before they could make the grand gesture that would involve flat-out rejection, I busied myself with something, anything, to divert their attention and make sure they saw I was incredibly interested in whatever that anything was and thoroughly uninterested in sex.

The puppy! I played with the puppy. What a cute puppy. Go fetch this thing I'll throw far from the bed, puppy. Oh, what a good puppy. That worked fine until the puppy hopped up on the bed and nestled next to Sheldon.

Great. Now what?

My markers! It just so happened Sheldon's bed was near a wall that had the crumbling remains of a fireplace. The rough bricks were long gone, leaving a smooth-ish surface of wall behind. The perfect canvas for a wall full of Rynski artwork.

Sheldon OK'ed the idea and I went to work. Drawing, coloring, swirling, shading, connecting, bisecting, circling – going wild with my artwork. I was up all night, until the sun started peeking through the filthy glass that remained in the windows.

I kept drawing and drawing and drawing, merrily fueled by the acid. Sunlight started streaming through the wooden slats nailed over the front window. A sound that was kind of like rain was coming from the back window, the one that faced the courtyard below.

The strange rain only lasted about less than a minute, and it came in a very narrow stream dribbling down what was left of the top window glass.

Oh. Someone on the floor above was peeing out their window and down into the central courtyard. I guess living without running water did have more than one drawback. I made a mental note to avoid the central courtyard.

Sheldon woke up and grinned like a sunbeam at my Rynski wall art. It was time for breakfast. Sheldon mentioned a Chinese take-out down the block. He also mentioned I should buy his meal.

I balked, thinking of my quickly dwindling $200 that was now easily down to the $150-ish range.

"Hey," he said, "I let you stay here. Got you acid. If you don't buy me breakfast, you're going to feel like a jerk every time you see me in the park and remember how you didn't buy me breakfast. You'll forever regret it."

Wow. He may be right. What if I ever needed him as a connection to get my own personal squat? Sigh. OK, fine.

Or maybe he meant it as a death threat? If I don't get his breakfast, I could end up as the next headline: "Michigan runaway murdered for refusing to buy beef and broccoli."

I bought him his meal.

Sheldon and I parted ways as I continued on my quest for Lon-Lan. An old man playing chess on a cement table in the park never heard of him. Another old man playing cards on a different cement table in the park didn't speak English.

Looking for this Lan dude was hard work. I better get another beer to think about my next move. That beer turned into another beer that turned into a third beer. You get the idea.

That was how it always went, if I had a say in it. From my earliest drinking days onward, all I remember was wanting more.

My mom once told me all the "more-ness" had started even earlier than my drinking. She'd read me a bedtime story when I was a toddler, but one was never enough.

"More, more!" I would shout, pointing for the next book, then the next.

More stories. More toys. More candy. More beer! I always wanted more, more, more!

By now it was dark out. I figured I'd have to try to sleep or I'd use up all my money on beer before the week was out. I laid down on the park bench and closed my eyes, visions of more dancing merrily through my head.

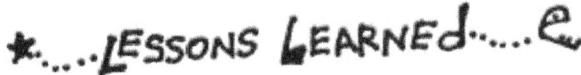
.....Lessons Learned.....

Make friends with strangers if you're living on the street.

Don't leave home without your markers.

Playing dumb has its benefits, as long as it doesn't become a way of life.

Skinheads and Fake Tattoos

All the days started blending together. Things just kind of happened. I bounced around smoking cigarettes, wearing my by-now itchy combat boots and asking anyone and everyone if they knew Lan.

I got pretty good at finding places to sleep that were better than the Tompkins Square Park wooden benches.

Vestibules were good in the rain, provided you could find a building with a broken lock or improperly shut front door. There were plenty of them.

The best one I found had a cubby hole behind the stairway, where I could crunch up and sleep in a fetal position. There was even a big rock near the front door that had been used to keep the door propped open. I tried using it as a pillow. Ouch.

Unmanned subway station entrances were OK in a pinch, but they had that same urine stench I first met at Port Authority. And you didn't want to go into squats by yourself, and not just because of Sheldon's warning. There were simply too many hiding places for all the drugged-out zombies.

The park bench at East River Park, in the no-man zone east of Avenue D, was probably the most dangerous place I tried to sleep. I had a feeling I knew why the place was deserted after dark. Even the junkies wouldn't go there.

As I was lying on the wooden green park bench, listening to the scuffle of rats in the nearby trash pile, a thought banged into my head like a gong.

Wow. Someone could come strangle me and no one would even know.

A tidbit of trepidation poked its way into my stomach.

Heck with this!

I got up from the bench and did what I always did when some type of emotion came through. Went to look for another beer. Drowned what I was feeling with a deluge of alcohol.

There. That's better. Back to the neutralized apathy.

While smothering emotions with beer kept my heart safe from hurt, it also kept it closed off from love. It kept It closed off from everything. Yet the same way I'm convinced drinking saved me from killing myself, I'm sure my apathy saved me from being beaten to a pulp – or even killed – on the night I encountered the skinheads.

Not sure if they were real skinheads or so-called posers, but you'd find little pockets of them hanging around Tompkins Square Park. Smoking cigarettes, wearing cuffed-up jeans to show off their combat boots. Sporting safety pins in their neck, ears and face. Red plaid shirt tied around their waist.

The same way a dog can smell fear, these guys sniffed out trouble. And if they couldn't find any, they'd make some. That's what they were trying to do when the found me on the sidewalk selling my little art plates in the middle of the night.

By this time, I had gotten pretty crafty when it came to getting money and food. I tried begging on a street corner when I saw others racking it up, but it took me more than an hour to get 50 cents. Not a good use of time and energy.

Collecting bottles and cans easily paid enough for the next beer or two, but the competition was fierce. You had to be quick to beat out all the other homeless folks who were doing the same. And the deposit was only a nickel per can.

So I instead started scouring trash piles for things I could turn into artwork. Unlike other areas of the world where the trash piles contain actual trash, New York City trash piles contain veritable treasures.

Tables. Chairs. Mirrors and picture frames. Piles of new-looking clothing (never my style). Competition was again cut-throat in the neighborhood in and around the park's homeless camp, but if you ventured a shade uptown a bit you could score some really fancy stuff.

Like the big crate of little plates I once found, perfect for making little Ryn-ified ashtrays. I broke out my markers, and whipped out a batch, drawing faces, skulls, bones, rats, demons or whatever other uplifting images came to mind.

Then I sat around on the street selling them. Business was slow, but I did sell a few. Although I lost quite a bit of investment when it started raining once and the marker started bleeding off the plates, smearing and running into a multicolored puddle.

While the obvious solution may have been to get permanent markers for my artwork, that would take away from my beer money. So I found an even better solution: Just don't try to sell them in the rain.

It was definitely non-rainy on the night I decided it would be a good idea to sell my little plates at around 2 a.m. on the deserted streets of Avenue B. Must have been yet another round of acid talking.

Since no one was around, business was zero. And I had plenty of time to break out my markers and draw all over the nearest thing.

The cops had already busted me once scrawling my "Ryn Rules" logo on a wall with my big, fat (permanent) graffiti marker.

They took away my marker and made me dump out my beer.

That meant drawing on the building façade behind me was not a good idea.

Hey. I was wearing shorts. And my legs looked so bare.

I spent the next stretch of time drawing swirls, skulls, circles, faces, flowers and jagged lines all up and down my legs. The more I drew, the cooler it looked.

Just when I was finishing off the artwork on my feet, a clunky black combat boot clomped down about an inch from my hand on the pavement. I looked up. There stood a whole band of those skinheads, grinning like jack-o-lanterns in a semi-circle around me.

Like I said, if they couldn't find trouble, they would go ahead and make some.

"What would you do if I smashed all these plates into little pieces and then started beating you to death?" snarled the guy who must have been the leader.

Good question, I thought. What would I do? Snapshots of scenarios flashed through my mind. I could cry and scream. I could run and hide. I could throw my body over my artwork in a last-gasp attempt to save my little plates.

I figured none of it would do any good if they were bent on beating me to death anyway.

And, to be honest, I didn't really care at that point if I lived or died. I had my answer.

I looked straight back into his steely eyes and told him my game plan: "I guess I would do nothing."

"Oh." He sat down next to me. "Could I bum a cigarette then?"

They all ended up sitting down around me, and we smoked and laughed and drank beer until the sun came up on the avenue.

⋆⋯⋯LESSONS LEARNED⋯⋯

People are less apt to kill you if you don't really care if you die.

Just because someone's looking for a fight doesn't mean you have to give it to them.

Two Men and a Dog

Living on the streets had its highlights for sure, but it could also get pretty itchy and tiresome. Especially in the sweltering summer when you're hauling around a heavy leather jacket and a body-sized duffel bag stocked with cassette tapes and markers.

I was back in Tompkins Square Park wondering what next, drinking my second or third beer of the day. A man with spikey white hair and crinkly eye wrinkles sat down next to me. He didn't know Lon, but he did have a pretty cool dog. A white Shar-Pei. It had short, spikey white hair and crinkly eye wrinkles.

Isn't there a thing that says people and their dogs end up looking like each other?

The man's name was Jax. His dog was Ghost. He lived right over there on Avenue A in the massive and clean-looking apartment building with a doorman.

He said I looked tired and dirty. I was. Did I want to come to his apartment and take a shower?

Believe it or not (I barely did), but Jax didn't attempt to kiss me, hug me or otherwise make any unseemly advances that would have most certainly resulted in me drawing all over his walls.

Even after the shower.

He instead explained how his place was a mess and he could use someone to help out, you know, cleaning the toilet and running to Key Food supermarket across the street when they were hungry. If I was game for it, I could stay at their studio apartment instead of sleeping on the streets.

No way. Not "no way" I didn't want this, but "no way," this is way too good to be true.

Was this how I'd meet my death, trusting a crinkly-wrinkly eye man? Hell with it. Let's try it and see what happens.

Since Jax didn't really have furniture, the place wasn't too tough to clean. There was a futon pad on the floor in the living room area and another pad on the floor where a kitchen table was probably meant to be. A big stereo system and couple of folding chairs rounded out the mix. That was it.

Oh, and there was also Big John. He wasn't really furniture, but he was as big as a couch and spent the day sleeping on the futon pad in the kitchen area. You had to be quiet when you swept around him.

He was Jax's roommate, a big black beefy bald bouncer. He could scare drunks enough to leave the bar with just the right sneer– but he was the biggest sweetheart to the ladies. I got to see his sweetheart side, at least if I didn't make him cranky.

After my chores and running to the grocery store for boxed macaroni and a six pack, I immediately grabbed one of the folding chairs and put it by the window. I popped open one of the beers and sat on the folding chair looking out the window.

For hours. Days.

The apartment was directly across the street from the Key Food. The entrance to Tompkins Square Park was a bit down the block. I was absolutely fascinated watching all the people swarm about, like ants, from six floors above.

I got to see arguments. Fights. Running. Hand-holding. And others just going about their errands, coming out of Key Food with plastic bags undoubtedly full of boxed macaroni and beer. That seemed to be the preferred diet of many living in and around Alphabet City.

I wondered what it would have been like to grow up here, in this exciting swirl of homeless tents and macaroni-eating city people. Everyone looked as unique as I did, with their own style on full display for the world to see. No cookie-cutter stuff around these parts.

I'll bet no one would have even blinked seeing a drunk teen lashing out at the cops or puking on the principal on homecoming game night.

Did they even have homecoming in New York City?

Everything was so different. So surreal. So strange. New York was definitely its own universe.

The nightlife was pretty cool when you didn't have to sleep outside in it. Big John would let me tag along when he went to work.

This was a thrill, of course, since it meant free beer. While he wouldn't let me come along when he worked in those clubs where everyone did Ecstasy and got naked, he did let me come along to Alcatraz.

No, not the haunted island prison in San Francisco. The dive bar on St. Marks Place and Avenue A. This corner bar was always packed with punks and drunks and ne'er do wells. I fit right in. I loved it. There were only two problems.

One was the juke box. I think it was broken. It had to be. For some reason it played Guns N' Roses "Sweet Child of Mine" again and again and again. Something like 802 times a night.

The other problem was the commitment. If I went with Big John on his shift, I would have to stay there the entire night until his shift was done around 2 a.m.

Jax usually spent nights out doing God knows what and I didn't have a key to the apartment. If I wanted to be in the apartment at all while they were out, I'd either have to stay inside the whole night or wait until one of them got home.

Sticking around the bar for the entire shift usually meant slamming free beers until I passed out in a back booth somewhere. Then Big John shaking me awake me when it was time to go home.

But one night we had to stay a little longer. Actually, everyone had to stay. We got locked in the bar, thanks to Big John's quick thinking. It was the night of the Tompkins Square Park riot of 1988.

Evidently the city wasn't as enthralled as I was about the tents, cardboard boxes, shopping carts and other homeless shelters in the park. And the yuppie element that had started invading the neighborhood was crying about the loud music and noises coming from the resident drug dealers and punks all night long.

While the city had a 1 a.m. curfew on all parks, it was never enforced at Tompkins Square. Until some brainiac decided it would be a good idea to do so. Come 1 a.m., everyone had to be cleared out. You could come back at dawn.

Good luck with that. It wasn't going so well during its first month, but police were showing up anyway, banging their Billy clubs on the park benches next to sleeping people's heads.

"Curfew. Time's up. Let's go."

Flyers taped on street lamps announced an Aug. 6 protest against the curfew. The homeless folks and squatters were joined by all kinds of activist types. As usual, some activists were for real and others were the type that show up at anything just to stir up trouble.

It was business as usual in Alcatraz. Drinks on the tables. Guns N' Roses on the juke box. People laughing and yelling. No one even seemed to know or remember a protest was scheduled that night – until a man's face went SPLAT against the front window.

He wasn't splatted like players against the Plexiglas at a hockey game. There was only a little blood, not a lot of blood. But his eye and cheek were flatted by the glass, like he was trying to make a funny face that ended up not being funny.

He had been pushed or thrown from behind.

Big John immediately scooted over to the bar's front door and bolted it shut.

"We're all going to hang out in here for a while," he said.

By then there was all kinds of screeching and banging and the sound of broken glass coming from the street. Grunting. Yelling. Pounding. Looters were throwing trash cans through the windows of nearby businesses and streaming in through the gaping holes.

"Get away from the front window," Big John told the bar people who ran up to take a look at what was going on.

Sirens. Wailing. Clomping. Thankfully, the bar window stayed intact and the mayhem stayed outside. So everyone pretty much went back to drinking as the riot roiled on into the night.

All had finally quieted down and we could go home. The street was a total mess. Overturned trash cans. Busted glass. Strewn trash. Sidewalks smeared with what looked like blood, vomit – or both.

Dang, I was so glad Big John locked the door.

Later reports said 38 were injured, a bunch of people were arrested for riot, assault and other charges, and there were either about 100 protestors or about 700 protestors – depending who you asked.

Police had ended up with a force of 450 officers, some on horseback. Riot gear. Police said the protestors started the violence by throwing bricks, rocks and firecrackers at them. Protesters said police just started beating on them for no given reason.

Injuries included a small handful of police officers and a bigger handful of protestors, reporters, and people who had nothing to do with the protest who just so happened to be in the wrong place at the wrong time. Six police brutality complaints were filed.

Mayor Ed Koch rescinded the curfew for the time being, saying the weather too hot and it made tempers flare. But he probably used different language.

Dang, I was so glad Big John locked the door.

Back in my comfy perch with my bottle of beer by the window, I was back to my favorite pastime of staring at Key Food customers across the street. But not for long.

"Hey! Hey Ryn!" Jax jostled me out of my reverie one afternoon. "You got company."

Company? Who the heck knew I was living in a studio apartment on Avenue A? Oh yeah! Dobie.

Remember him? The moldy cheese pizza boy. We had been in touch, planning his arrival. He finally made it.

I figured we'd both be able to crash with Big John and Jax, keeping this cushy lifestyle going. I was wrong.

"He can take a shower here and store his stuff here," Jax said, "but he can't stay here."

Dobie took his shower. He put his duffel bag and electric typewriter in the closet next to my body-bag sized sack of markers. He came here to make it as a writer. I wondered where he was expecting to plug in his electric typewriter. Then the two of us were back on the street.

While it was great to see Dobie at first, the weariness of having nowhere to sleep tends to get to you after a while. Especially when you were giving up the luxury of Big John's futon, the one he left vacant all night while out doing his bouncer work at bars and clubs.

There was tension between me and Dobie from the start. It felt like one of those friendships where you know the two of you have grown in separate directions but you remain friends anyway because you feel like you have to.

I was so done with the street living and the futile quest for the non-existent Lan-Lon, but it was all new to Dobie. He hated it immediately. He grumbled and groaned. Cried his leather jacket was way too heavy and hot – but he didn't trust leaving it up in Jax's place. Not only that, but his combat boots were giving him blisters.

Unlike my take of the New York experience where I was at least going to pretend to like it no matter what, he didn't. He made it distinctly clear it was all a real big pain in the ass.

Oh yeah, and three other Michigan pals also knew about the Avenue A studio. One was a guy who had been a boyfriend, who I still felt a connection to. The other two were his friends who he talked into driving him to the East Village. They were expected to arrive for a visit any day now.

If Jax didn't want one surly teenage dude from Michigan staying in the apartment, he certainly wouldn't welcome three more. He didn't. Didn't even offer the shower for these three. At least they could park their car in front of the apartment building.

So there we were, a gaggle of five Michigan teens sitting on a Tompkins Square park bench, drinking beer. Or at least I was. I don't think the rest of them had such a yearning to drink every minute of every day.

As long as I had my beer, I was happy. It didn't matter where I was. The others were more aligned with Dobie's thinking: It's hot. We're hungry. Everything smells like urine. This is supposed to be fun?

Once night started to fall, so did the rain. Dobie and two of the pals went to sleep in the car. That left me and boyfriend guy on the streets in the rain. We needed a rain-sleeping spot that was big enough for two.

Someone had finally fixed the lock on my favorite vestibule building, so that was out. All my other hiding spots were only big enough for one. I decided to ignore Sheldon's early warning and go ferret out a squat where we could at least spend the night. As long as we avoided Sheldon's building, maybe we'd be OK.

We crawled into one building or another, found a vacant apartment on an upper floor that no one was living in, and called it home. Once it started raining even harder, it was apparent why no one had picked this apartment to live in. Rain was blasting through most of the ceiling, leaving a small dry spot near a corner.

We huddled in that corner, lit the candles we picked up at the nearby bodega. We put them on cider blocks we had found, although there probably wasn't much chance of a fire with all that rain coming in.

I had also taken a cue from Sheldon and propped a big, loud piece of metal in front of the door. It didn't have padlocks, but it did block most of the doorway.

Don't ask me why, but I remember feeling cozy and excited. Perhaps it was the prospect of having my very own New York City apartment, at least for a night, even though it rained inside it. Even though the place was strewn with massive piles of musty-smelling garbage.

Like the slummy buildings in Detroit that made me feel comfortable, I was once again on the same wavelength as my dismal surroundings. My outsides needed to match my insides, and my insides were apparently leaky and stuffed with all kinds of mushy trash.

In our little huddled corner with the candles flickering and the rain streaming through the ceiling, we eventually fell asleep.

BANG. BOING. CRASH BAM CRASH CRASH.

The sound of someone or something kicking in the metal over the doorway woke us up with a jolt. Flashlights were blasted in our faces, followed by more kicking noises.

"Whaddya doin' in here, living like pigs – get outta here. Get up, get outta here!"

Eeek! I thought for sure it was the squat people police, the stuff Sheldon had warned about. I was sure they were ready to kill us for squatting in an apartment without going through the proper channels of hierarchy and authority.

My heart was beating out of my chest, terrified of what the squat people police might do to us.

But I need not have worried. It wasn't the squat people police at all. It was the New York City police. They were rousting all the homeless out of the condemned building for whatever reason right before dawn.

What luck. We picked the one building in the entire collection of dilapidated buildings that the city was actually doing something about. We were shuttled out into the street in the early morning light, along with dozens of other people who had been sleeping inside the building shell.

Dang, there were a lot of us. I remember a photo journalist coming around, taking people's pictures. Boyfriend guy and I made funny faces, so I bet ours didn't make the front page.

We met up with Dobie and the two other pals for a breakfast somewhere. Then the two pals wanted to go back to Michigan as rapidly as humanly possible. We got back to their car to find someone had jimmied open and stolen everything from the trunk. Out-of-state plates apparently draw thieves to the trunk like rats to a plate of spaghetti sauce.

I don't even think they waved goodbye. I don't think they ever came back.

It was once again one of those hot muggy mornings with Dobie being cranky and hating every minute of our big exciting adventure. I don't recall what we were fighting about, but we were yelling at each other in Tompkins Square Park.

The yelling turned to top-of-the-lung screaming turned to Dobie hurling his leather jacket in my face. The clunky zipper hit me in the chin. Ouch.

I turned and saw the notorious semi-circle of skinheads behind us. I caught the eye of the leader and immediately demanded:

"Kick his ass!"

They did. And hard. So hard I couldn't watch. I slithered away into the distance, most likely going to get a beer.

When I came back to check on Dobie, he was gone. I checked all our hangouts. He was gone. Damn. I felt awful. I had only spouted out the demand in a moment of extreme anger. I didn't really want him to get beat up. Or disappear.

These were the days before cell phones so it's not like I could just sent a happy little "Where are you?" text. I envisioned all kinds of horrible scenarios. He was in the hospital. He was in the morgue. He was bleeding to death on the subway tracks.

I looked for him for days, but never found him. I instead found something far worse.

✱·····LESSONS LEARNED······℮

Don't ask a band of skinheads to beat someone up unless you really mean it.

New York City isn't for everyone.

Two Men and a Bathtub

"You look like you lookin' for someone," a voice from behind said. It came from a scrawny dude with Jheri curls, those greasy-looking ringlets that were all the rage in the 1980s.

No, he didn't know Lan-Lon. No, he hadn't seen a beat-up surly teen from Michigan limping around in combat boots. And no, he didn't have any money he could give me to buy some beer.

But he knew a way I could get beer.

"How's that?"

One of his friends owned a jewelry store and she needed someone to work there.

I had no money and didn't feel like going back to Jax and Big John at the moment. Since Jax made me leave when my pals came, I was going to show them I could find something even better. So there.

"Let me see this jewelry store and meet this friend," I said.

The jewelry-store friend was some cool-looking chick. The store was packed with huge, obnoxious dangly earrings. That was good enough for me.

"When do I start?"

Not only did I get a place to work, but Jheri curls happened to live in the apartment above the jewelry store with one of his other pals. This pal was a fat man with about 14 chins. Together, Jheri-curl slim man and fat man reminded me of Laurel and Hardy.

How can Laurel and Hardy be dangerous?

Besides, I figured it must be a New York runaway thing, where random New Yorkers would offer the kind of setup I had with Jax. I'd clean the bathroom and go buy boxed macaroni. They'd give me beer and lodging. With a bonus jewelry store income.

I thought wrong.

Once in their clutches upstairs, they immediately snatched up my small purse-bag thing I had with me and put it in the closet. Then they said I needed a makeover.

They cut my hair. Talked about dying it a different color. The fat one wanted to give me a bath in the clawfoot tub that was sitting in the middle of the apartment.

Bath tubs in the middle of the world is an old-time New York City thing. I cringed at the thought of getting in it, of his meaty hands touching my naked flesh. I wanted to vomit.

"You look just like Marilyn Monroe," he told me.

I knew Marilyn Monroe as blonde, smiling and gorgeous. I was brunette, scowling and scruffy.

But yeah, whatever.

That wasn't the only lie I caught them in. They promised I could work at the jewelry shop in exchange for money and beer, but once they had me upstairs they didn't let me go anywhere.

I was under their watch 24/7. Even slept on a futon on the floor with the fat man's meaty arm thrown across my chest. The front door had about four deadbolts. The second-floor windows had bars on them.

They gave me food and water, sure. Chinese take-out and such. But the beer was not forthcoming. At all.

"You promised me beer," I'd insist.

"Here, try these pills instead."

"No, you said I could have beer."

"This here will make you feel even better than beer," showing me a needle.

"I don't want your drugs. Where's my beer."

I finally wore them down enough to buy me a wine cooler. A single wine cooler.

This place was a horror. And for perhaps the first time on my grand New York adventure, I had a tinge of real fear. They locked away my possessions. Kept me trapped in this apartment. Cut my hair. Were trying to get me hooked on drugs.

Damn. I gotta get outta here. I don't want to die as a no-name statistic.

Since my head was without beer, I could actually think. Fat man was the weak link, always getting scolded by slim man for something or other. Laurel and Hardy for sure.

I told fat man I needed my purse-bag thing because it was that time of the month (it wasn't). He got me my bag. I went in the bathroom and pretended to do what I needed to do.

I made sure to put the purse-bag thing nonchalantly near the closet, but not in it, and then distract him with something. The bag was strategically situated for an easy grab, on the pathway between the futon we slept on and the front door.

"Can we play cards?"

"No. It's time to go to sleep."

As usual, slim man was either in the bedroom with the door closed or out gallivanting around all night, probably trying to find more runaway teens they could turn into Marilyn Monroe.

Also as usual, fat man laid down next to me on the futon, with his ham hock of an arm thrown across my chest. I waited. He started snoring. I wiggled out from underneath the ham hock arm and waited some more.

The little red clock next to my head said something like 2:32 a.m. He snores were deeper and louder. Now or never. I made my move.

I scampered up, grabbed my purse-bag thing, unlocked the deadbolts on the door and bolted down the stairs out of the building. That was the fastest I've moved. Ever. Even beat out my soccer-playing speeds or my middle school track days jumping hurdles.

My heart was racing 900 miles a minute. I made it back to the park, catching my breath. I sat in an open area where I'd be sure to see them coming from all sides, just in case I needed to run some more.

A big figure started approaching me from the distance. I was just getting ready to get up and run, but the big figure's voice stopped me.

"Holy mackerel. Look who's here!" It was Big John, asking where I had been all this time. I'd tell him later. For now, heading back to the Jax-Big John setup sounded great.

We walked in the apartment, Big John announcing my arrival to Jax:

"Hey Jax, look what the cat dragged in!"

It was nice to know I had been missed.

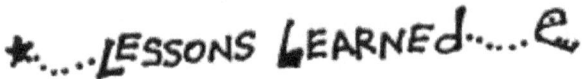

Don't fall for false flattery or empty promises.

Always make note of the exits. And how to unlock the door.

Porno Ice Cream

After all that drama with Jheri curl and Hardy, I was ready to get back into my usual routine: sitting on the folding chair, drinking beer and staring out the window at Key Food. But this time Big John and Jax weren't having it.

"Here," Jax said, handing me a ratty scrap of paper with an address scrawled on it. "We ran across this ice cream shop that's hiring. It's time for you to go get a job."

The ice cream shop was owned by two brothers, and luckily the nice-guy brother was the one who interviewed me. He hired me on the spot. Nitpicky brother would come to the shop, unannounced, trying to catch the employees doing something wrong.

My first interaction with him was him running to the drug store to buy a nail brush.

"You can't touch people's ice cream cones with nails looking like that," he said while handing me the nail brush.

It's not my fault dirt likes to collect beneath them, geesh.

The second interaction was something about a thing called wainscoting.

"Who was in charge of dusting today? You need to do the wainscoting."

I didn't even know what the heck wainscoting was, how was I supposed to know to dust it?

The third interaction was monumental enough to make a wholesale change across the entire shop. I had been wearing one of my usual tank tops, one of my favorites actually. It was a beat-up semi-see-through white thing with some evil eagle or something on the front.

My black bra was clearly visible through the tank, except where the evil eagle emblem was, and the straps were hanging out the back and sides. This was before that look was supposed to be cool. It was just skanky.

Nitpicker brother walked in, saw my shirt, and had a conniption.

"What is this, porno ice cream?!" he screamed.

Nitpicker ushered me to the back of the shop immediately, handing me a giant, royal blue ice cream shop apron. It reached up to my neck and down to the middle of my thighs.

Everyone was given shop T-shirts to wear as a uniform thereafter.

Yeah, nitpicky brother had his hands full for sure, at least when Vinnie and I were working. Vinnie was the shop manager, a muscular, smiling sparkplug of a guy that everyone loved.

Customers loved him especially, since he was the generous type. He'd serve up a single scoop of ice cream that was as big as a house. When it was just us working, he'd also blast the music loud enough to shake the life-size wooden cow cut-outs.

Neither habit went over well when nitpicky showed up one day.

"What is this, is a disco?!"

We could barely hear what nitpicky was saying over the blaring rock n' roll. But his face was all red and veiny – so you could tell he was really angry. He got angrier still when he saw the massive mountain of ice cream Vinnie just sold as a single scoop.

A new music rule went into effect that day, something about volume levels not going above three. Nitpicky also bought one of those little food scales people use when they're dieting. From now on we had to weigh each scoop of ice cream we sold. A single scoop was not to weigh more than 6 ounces.

And yes, there were video cameras throughout the shop. Nitpicky would go into the back office and watch our actions at the front counter. He probably took the other tapes home to watch them, making sure we had clean nails, dusted wainscoting, low levels of music, proper attire and just the right size ice cream scoops.

Thank God I worked mainly with Vinnie, and sometimes with the laid-back brother. Other times I had to put up with Krissie, the oh-so-perfect New York University student with a little blond bob and little high-pitched voice.

She was nitpicky's favorite. She was also as dumb as a stump.

One evening a zombie-like man in a dirty beige raincoat came shuffling into the shop. Even though we were in NYU territory, scruffy customers were not uncommon. It was New York City in the late 1980s, after all.

Vinnie was back in the office. Krissie was meticulously wiping hot fudge off the back counter. I was front and center, ready to take scruffy man's order.

He plopped a folded newspaper on the counter and asked for a vanilla cone with chocolate sprinkles.

I turned around to make his cone, diligently weighing the single scoop of vanilla and making sure to use only a single tablespoonful of sprinkles.

When I turned back around to hand the man his cone, I instead dropped it on the floor in shock. I think I also peed my pants.

That's because he had a gun nestled in the folded-up newspaper and it was pointed directly at my face.

"Open the register," he barked. "Gimme the money!"

"Uh, umm…ahhh…" I was trying to stall as I hit the secret red button beneath the counter, the one that supposedly alerted the cops that we needed immediate help.

Krissie ran over to the register and opened it, grabbing all the wads of cash that were visible in the drawer. This was a pretty hopping ice cream shop, so the guy got thick piles of singles, fives and tens. All the bigger bills were hidden beneath the cash drawer.

He grabbed the cash and turned to leave. I began to breathe a big sigh of relief. He was halfway to the front door. That's when Krissie screamed out to him, calling him back.

"Wait!," she said in her little mouse voice as she lifted up the cash drawer. "Don't you want the twenties?!"

Both nitpicky and nice brother rushed to the shop as soon as Vinnie called to tell them what happened. They beat the cops' arrival by about two hours. So much for the immediate assistance button. But then again, it was New York in the late 1980s. Police were pretty busy.

The brothers took us out to buy us drinks to calm our nerves. They evidently didn't realize who they had just offered free drinks to. I could easily rack up a bar bill that was about five times what the scurffy man stole.

I think Krissie ordered something and tonic and was tipsy after a few sips. I was slamming whatever they were buying as fast as it could be served.

"You must be shaken up from the robbery," nice brother said as he watched me guzzling drink after drink.

"Yes, very," I said. Whatever. I don't remember if Krissie every came back to work but I do remember they never offered employees free drinks again.

Vinnie was used to my drinking. He didn't even flinch when I was once dropped off for work in a limousine, thanks to whatever get-paid-with-a-limousine deal Jax had been working on at the time. A limousine stocked with endless champagne.

When I stumbled out of the limo and into work evening, swirling and laughing, I had absolutely no clue what was going on. At least I wasn't late. Or at least I don't think I was. I don't remember. In fact, I didn't remember much of anything.

I woke up with my face next to gushy wet mop. The mop was swishing back and forth. I rolled over and realized I was lying on the tile floor in the back room, where they kept all the extra ice cream and giant cans of fudge. The ice cream shop was closed. Vinnie was mopping up the back so he could lock the shop and go home.

Oops. Vinnie had covered my entire shift, was even doing the mopping. That was definitely an underling's job. He even gave me all the money out of the little paper coffee cup by the register with the hand-written "Tips" sign. Usually it got split among whomever was working that night.

That's the kind of guy he was. Friendly and smiling to all. He also worked as a waiter and bartender at other jobs, earning about $9 million a night in tips. Everyone loved Vinnie.

Well, except maybe that band of thugs we had run into one Sunday in front of a bank not far from Chinatown. I don't remember how the fight started, but I know I started it. Sadly, that was one of my M.O.s. I'd get drunk, mouth off, and start fights.

Yes, I've gotten my ass kicked. Bad. But that was only if I was by myself. If I was with a guy, as I was that Sunday afternoon with Vinnie, the offended party would start beating on the guy.

In this case, there were three guys. Maybe four. I seemed to subconsciously always start trouble when I was either grossly outweighed or outnumbered. In this case it was outnumbered.

Vinnie was sturdy as a fire hydrant and muscular as hell. The four thugs descended on him, one by one, like a Kung Fu movie but backwards. Instead of the Chinese guys having all kinds of fancy moves that outsmarted their opponents, Vinnie took each one of them on with brute force and perfect aim.

They faltered. They fell. They went down like bowling pins. When the last guy came at him, Vinnie grabbed him, fast, before the dude knew what was happening. And he hurled him right through the ceiling-to-floor plate glass bank window, setting off the alarm.

A giant SMASH of glass, then the high-pitched wail of the security alarm.

Everybody scattered, like cockroaches when you turn on the light. Except the guy who got thrown the window. He was still lying there, abandoned by his posse.

We didn't stick around to see what happened, but I know from that point on, Vinnie was a guy I could trust with my life.

*.....LESSONS LEARNED......

You can spot-check an eatery's cleanliness by checking for dust on the wainscoting.

Don't start fights you can't finish. You might not always have a Vinnie.

No matter if or where you go to college, you can still be as dumb as a stump.

Ninth and C

Jax turned wishy-washy. Or maybe he was always wishy-washy but it just didn't matter. Now it did. He was kicking us out of the apartment.

The us in this case was me and Big John. The reason behind the sudden eviction was a guy named Alfonso. Alfonso was a sickly-looking, shaved-head man who wore pointy shiny shoes and crisply pleated pants.

Big John said he knew the eviction was coming because he heard Jax and Alfonso whispering. Alfonso had some shady scheme of sorts that would make them a bunch of money, but "the big guy and the weird chick have to go."

As if getting kicked out the cushy arrangement wasn't bad enough, Alfonso had also taken it upon himself to steal anything of mine he wanted before they gave me and Big John the boot.

Say goodbye to Dobie's electric typewriter and most of my really cool markers.

Say hello to living in some of the seediest so-called hotels New York City had to offer. If you can even call them hotels. Although the word "hotel" was in most of their names, like the St. Mark's Hotel across from Munchie's Deli, they were not places that would be listed as options in tourist brochures.

More like haunted tour brochures. Places where you really didn't know what you'd find if you sprayed the rooms with luminal.

But hey, Big John was paying for the rooms and bringing home beer and sometimes drugs from his bouncing gigs. And it was better than sleeping on the street. Just barely.

Even though seedy places usually made me feel right at home, these were below even my low standards. I think it was because people automatically assumed I was a hooker.

Yeah, most were the type of places that were typically rented for an hour, not as a home. And the leers from the old toothless men from behind the counter creeped me out right down to the marrow.

The St. Mark's Hotel was the biggest wormhole on the East Side.

We also stayed at a West Side dump of a place right next to the West Side Highway. At least the surrounding neighborhood had ambiance and class. It was right next to the blood-soaked meat packing district. And you thought the smell of urine was bad. Try the stench of rotting meat.

Only one hotel stood out as a little different. Some artsy place on 20-something street where every room had a different theme. I knew this because we lived in a enough of them. One room would be bright pink with red swirls. Another would be aqua blue with stars and moons all over the place.

Like most hotels in this part of New York City, the bathroom was down the hall, shared by everyone on the floor. I remember a crotchety old man who once locked himself in there so long I had to go to a different floor to use their bathroom.

One evening, the whole hallway was wet from water seeping out from under the bathroom door. Big John and I theorized the old man must have hit his head while filling the tub, letting it overflow into oblivion while his dead body bobbled and weaved in the flooded bathroom.

I wrote a poem about it called "Crotchety, Grickly Old Man."

There was a "Do Not Use" sign on the bathroom door the next day.

Another rule in these types of hotels was the length of time you were allowed to live there. You could only stay there for something like 28 days before you had to move out for at least a day before you could come back again.

Some kind of something about tenant laws or whatever. So we moved from here and there, there and here, me carting around my new pet rat in a cage and fending off the sickly leers from old men who thought I was a hooker.

"Good news, Ryn!" Big John was ecstatic. "I got us a place to live."

Ended up a friend of a friend he knew through his big circle of acquaintances knew a guy who managed a building on East Ninth Street and Avenue C. Perfect location for him to get to his main bouncing gig on Avenue A.

Perfect anything just to get out of these damn hotels.

"Yaay!"

Visions of a super cool apartment began dancing in my head. An actual kitchen with an actual refrigerator. No more warm beer! Two bedrooms. A family room. A bathroom that was inside the apartment, not down the hall with a drowned old man floating around in it.

We packed up our bags, said good riddance to the hotel clerk, and tromped our way down to Ninth Street and Avenue C.

Remember those squats where my first New York pal Sheldon lived, or where former-boyfriend boy and I stayed when we were yelled at by cops for living like pigs?

The building looked like one of those, just missing the "Condemned" sign across it. Well, this was a little better. The windows actually had glass in them. There was a front door that opened and closed, so we didn't have to climb through the basement window.

And, of course, the big difference. We had to pay to live there. Even though it was connected to a friend of a friend of an acquaintance of someone, squats were the only places you got to live for free.

The first thing Big John warned me about were the zombies. The building was next to a vacant field, littered with debris.

The same type of junkies that lived behind mattresses in the Sheldon building basement also lived behind the debris.

The zombies had yellow eyes and shuffled around. Don't let them come shuffling up to you, God only knows what could happen then. I thought of the semi-zombie that robbed us in the ice cream shop. Yep. Stay away from the zombies.

The second thing he warned me about was the building's super, Carlos. Carlos was bordering on a different type of junkie-ism. Unlike the heroin zombies that shuffled about, Carlos was wound up like a tangled marionette.

Damn crack.

Carlos led us up the stairs to the second-floor apartment we could stay in. One thing nobody mentioned – it already had a tenant. A listless man who was sitting on the mottled brown carpet in the back bedroom watching a fuzzy black-and-white TV.

Big John quickly dubbed the guy Norman Bates.

"You guys can have the front bedroom," Carlos said as he left. Norman Bates was no problem. Mainly because he vanished after a week or so. We didn't even notice at first. He left his TV behind. I moved it into the front bedroom.

Big John examined the apartment's front door, showing me how to prop a big metal stick against it when I was home. The stick had an anchor point in the floor, a built-in metal bar in a hole in the suffering linoleum.

The front bedroom had the same mottled brown carpet as the back bedroom. The window above the radiator was painted open about five inches, so it got plenty of fresh air. Or at least outside air.

I set up my pet rat on a shelf on the radiator, artfully arranging his little bowl of food and little bowl of water. My rats were allowed to live on shelves off the floor. They always came back to their home base, so I never worried about them running away.

The bathroom was in the apartment, as envisioned. There was a kitchen and fridge, not really as envisioned. Most people wouldn't envision a beat-up old hulk of a fridge built around 1959.

But at least it was better than a hotel. Or so I thought for a moment, before the horror began.

The first episode of horror at Ninth and C came when I was sitting on the toilet and heard screeching from a few feet to my right. The screeching was coming from the shower area, which was blocked off from view from one of those half-walls that separate the shower and the toilet.

I figured I must be hearing things. But it just got louder.

"Screech! Screech! Screech!"

I craned my neck around the half-wall to see what the heck was going on.

Eeek! It looked like a fight to the death.

Two gargantuan sewer rats were battling it out on the shower floor, propped up on their hind legs and facing each. If it had not been so horrifying, it might have been funny. I saw the shower drain had no cover, explaining how they got in there.

If rats can fit their tiny little heads through an opening, they can elongate their bodies to get through. And the shower drain pipe was kind of fat to begin with.

"Screech! Screech! Screech!"

I flushed and scurried from the bathroom, making a note to never stand straddling the drain when taking a shower. I made another note not to sit all the way down on the toilet. And to always do my business as fast as possible.

The sewer rats didn't confine themselves to the bathroom.

"Keep the bread in the fridge," Big John told me. "I saw rats on the counter, munching away on it. And I found little loaves all over the kitchen floor."

"Little loaves" was Big John slang for rat poop.

None of the loaves were from my own pet rat. He stayed in the bedroom, living on his little shelf beneath the painted-open window.

But I did notice his white coat was getting a little dirtier. And he wasn't as friendly as he used to be, being quite stand-offish. I found out why one night when I went to play with him but he wasn't on his shelf.

Where the heck could he be?

I caught a flash of white outside the window. He was on a ledge right outside the window – running back and forth with one of the neighborhood sewer rats.

Great. No wonder he wasn't as friendly. No wonder his food bowl was perpetually empty. He was making friends with all the neighborhood rats, bringing them back to eat and play.

Although I wouldn't say he was necessarily responsible for the bread-eaters or the shower-boxing rats, I agreed with Big John that he had to go. We couldn't just let him loose. He was already loose and bringing his friends over.

Dammit.

Big John took on the task of putting him to sleep. I went in the other room so I didn't have to watch. He said the rat screamed bloody murder when he stuck a pin into his brain.

Thankfully, I didn't hear it. I cried and still cringe at the whole scenario.

Dammit. Dammit. Dammit.

I didn't get another pet rat for some time. I had to recover from this one.

Drinking a beer would make it better.

A near heart attack was another thing I had to recover from during my time at Ninth and C. One night as I was sleeping, there was a massive bang on the front window of the front bedroom.

This wasn't the painted-open window. That one was on the side. This window was facing the street. The window with the fire escape.

BANG. BANG. BANG.

It's the zombie junkies!

No, they wouldn't have the strength to bang that loudly.

It's my pet rat coming back from the dead!

No, why would he bang? He knew all about the painted-open window. Besides, rat ghosts can go through walls if they want to.

BANG BANG BANG.

It's a mass murderer coming to get me!

I crunched down under the covers on the top bunk of the old bunk bed in the room. I heard the window creaking open. I heard the slithering of a person coming inside.

I grabbed the nearest thing I could find, the only thing near me up here on the top bunk. An empty beer can. Yeah, I'll hit him in the head with an empty beer can.

"Hey, it's Carlos," said the voice. "I need the rent money."

"Big John isn't here," I said, trying to sound all tough and fearless, as if a crazy crackhead breaking into my bedroom in the middle of the night didn't make me blink an eye. "I have no money. I'll tell him you stopped by."

He slipped back out the window and left. I had a feeling it was time to move.

....LESSONS LEARNED.....

Keep weapons more powerful than an empty beer can next to your bed.

Street rats and pet rats don't mix.

Just because you pay for something doesn't mean it's good.

Chicken Man Dan

Carlos. Norman Bates. The zombies next door. Yeah, the Ninth and C building was packed with all kinds of joy. Especially since our upstairs neighbor was Chicken Man Dan.

I remembered Chicken Man Dan from my sleeping-in-the-park days. He was a regular around Tompkins Square Park. Seemed everyone around the Lower East Side knew who he was.

He had that grungy Jesus look you see in some wanna-be cult leaders, although this guy's cult membership was pretty low. It was just himself.

His nickname came from the dried-up chicken claw he wore around his neck.

Chicken Man Dan would always invite me to smoke a joint with him in the park. Now I'd see him hanging around outside the building, inviting me to smoke weed and hang out in his apartment.

Something always told me not to.

I discovered what that something was when I came home one day to find news vans all over the block, reporters swarming around the building. When I got upstairs, Big John was jumping up and down in front of the little black-and-white TV.

"He's on the news, Ryn. He's on the news!"

"Who's on the news?"

"Chicken Man Dan!"

Sure enough, the fuzzy picture on the little TV was showing live coverage of our building with a photo of Chicken Man Dan in the corner of the screen. The caption said "Accused Killer."

Wha?!

Although I had never seen him with a woman, Chicken Man Dan evidently had a girlfriend. That he killed upstairs during an argument.

To get rid of evidence, he allegedly boiled her bones in a pot on the stove, then flushed her remains down the toilet. That means they had been swirling around the pipes in the very building in which I lived.

Ew. And I thought rats in the shower pipes were bad.

The story got even more grotesque, with reports eventually saying he didn't flush the remains, but made them into a soup to feed the homeless in the park. Then it was just her head that was boiled, making the soup from her brains.

Whatever the case, her skull was found in a bucket in the bag check facility of Port Authority. And Chicken Man Dan got a not guilty by reason of insanity.

I looked him up years later, Daniel Rakowitz. Found a report with more details on his relationship with murder victim Monika Beerle, a 26-year-old modern dancer from Switzerland who was looking for a place to live when she met Daniel.

Apparently Monika was just pretending to be his girlfriend so she could get her name on the lease and steal the apartment out from under him. When her plot started to unfold, so did his rage. So he strangled her.

Since the 1991 verdict, Chicken Man Dan has remained locked up at Kirby Forensic Psychiatric Center on Wards Island, a maximum-security facility for the criminally insane.

✱.....LESSONS LEARNED......€

Always trust your gut, no matter how full of beer it may be. Instincts are messages from above.

Don't date dudes who have dried-up chicken claws around their neck.

Kicking and Screaming

"That's enough of that," ice cream manager Vinnie said when I told him the Chicken Man Dan story. "I'm going to find you a new place to live."

And he did. A studio apartment on Stanton Street, still in the downtown zone but not as far down as Tompkins Square Park – both figuratively and literally.

It was a tiny box of an apartment with a huge bathroom. I moved in with a futon and the black-and-white TV Big John was generous enough to give me as a parting gift. I found a milk crate that worked as a TV table.

That was it.

I also got a new job, a full-time gig at the big chain of pet shops throughout the tristate area. I figured since I loved animals, it would be a perfect match. But I failed the test miserably the first time I applied.

How was I supposed to know they'd be asking about live-breeders and egg-laying fish?

I went to the library to study, remembering most of the questions. I made sure a different manager was on duty when I went back to apply again, this time armed with all the right answers.

But I made a faux pas that made it obvious I had simply memorized the stuff from a book. While people who were actually familiar with fish would have put answers like mollies for the live-breeders and tetra for the egg-layers, I put the fancy Latin names that came from the fish encyclopedia.

The manager in charge looked at my test and sent me way downtown to a location across from City Hall. The manager there kind of smirked when he read my answers.

Dang. He was on to me.

But then he asked me a single question that I knew would make or break his decision to hire me.

"You put 'Heterandria' as a live-bearing fish," he said. "But what's the common name for Heterandria?"

Dang times two. Wait! I know this. I remember reading this. I know this. I know this.

"Mosquito fish!" I blurted out. Yes, yes, yesssss!

The Heterandria is the mosquito fish. The Heterandria is the mosquito fish! I pulled that one out of a hat in my head somewhere.

I could start my new job next Monday.

Even with the $9 million a night in tips, Vinnie found it tough to keep footing the monthly bill for my apartment. Even though I was working full-time, I was still only making minimum wage. I couldn't afford the shoe box studio on my own.

Great. I needed to find a new place to live.

When I was moaning about my situation to my pet shop boss, he had an ideal solution. Why not move in with him and his fiancé. Wow. I could live with Larry and Diane, rent free, until I saved enough for me own place. Cool! But there was a catch. Two, actually.

One was that they lived in Brooklyn. Egads. One of the reasons I ran away to New York City was so I could have a New York, New York address. Not a Brooklyn, New York address. (Never mind that the majority of my time so far had been with NO address.)

If I wanted a New York, New York, address I had to live in Manhattan. Brooklyn, New York, is still technically part of New York City – it's made up the five boroughs of Manhattan, Brooklyn, the Bronx, Staten Island and Queens.

But still. It says "Brooklyn" not "New York" on the envelope. Kicking and screaming, I agreed to Brooklyn.

The second catch was even more horrifying. It was one he proposed after I moved in with the couple and he saw how much I drank. And drank. And drank. He smoked pot like it was going out of style, but that was different.

He would ration my alcohol to two beers a day. Sigh. I honestly tried it for a while. But all the two beers did was make me want two more. So I figured out a workaround. I was "allowed" two beers in the evening at his apartment.

I would just make sure not to go straight there after work, to make up some excuse that I had to do this and that and would be there later. That way we didn't have to take the subway together from work back to his apartment, since he would count the two beers on the train as part of my quota.

My new habit was to grab a few beers and hang out at the nearby City Hall Park after dark. The deli across the street from the park sold beer. They also sold hotdogs and spaghetti sauce, which I found out the giant rats at the park absolutely loved.

I was fascinated by the giant rats. As long as they weren't slithering up my shower drain or making friends with my own pets, these creatures were thoroughly fascinating. Smart as all get-out. Tough enough to live through anything. If I had to be an animal, I would be a rat.

Maybe one in City Hall Park, so I could dine on hotdogs and spaghetti sauce.

Except for the two-beer rule, all was going OK living with my boss in the middle of Brooklyn. Big John was just a memory. Vinnie and I still kept in touch; we hung out from time to time. And Larry's friend Morty was smart and funny.

Morty came around a lot. He and Larry would talk fish. Both worked in pet shops forever. Larry even had multiple aquariums set up in his apartment, where he bred or did whatever with all types of specimens.

He also kept two-liter bottles of urine in his fridge, something to do with the whatever part.

As I got to know Morty better, I was really starting to like him. He was currently living with his mother. Didn't drink at all. Wore a silver bracelet with the Serenity Prayer on it. That made him an even better pal. I didn't have to share my beer!

Besides, when Morty was over, Larry was distracted. He stopped counting how many beers I was drinking. I got friendlier with Morty. He got friendlier with me. One day Larry caught us making out in the bathroom.

"Well look at that," Larry joked. "Why don't you two move in together?"

So we did.

*.....LESSONS LEARNED......e

Trying to limit alcohol intake for an alcoholic doesn't make them a non-alcoholic. It just makes them cranky.

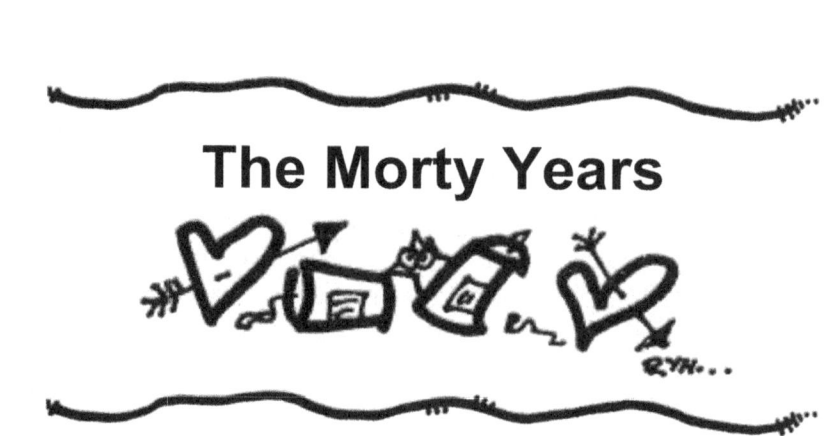

The Morty Years

Thus began a 12-year love affair. Not necessarily between me and Morty. I loved him the best I could, but something else had already captured my heart. That something was beer.

"I'd never ask you to choose between me and alcohol," Morty once told me. "I know which one you'd pick."

And he was right. Once out of Larry's scrutinizing beer limit, and a double full-time income coming into the home, it was off the drinking races, big time. So much so, that Morty soon joined the fun.

Morty began drinking as much as I did.

We made sure the drinking came with fun and games – without even trying.

One of the greatest evenings of fun came on the way to see the "Brady Bunch Live" play in Manhattan. Morty and I were on the overhead subway platform near our Brooklyn apartment, sipping our cans of brown-bagged beers for the road and waiting for the train to come.

I had my back to the train as it was pulling into the station. I glanced behind me to see the side of the train and, thinking the train had fully stopped, I reached my arm back behind me to lean on it.

But the train had still been moving. Instead of connecting with the side of the train car, my outstretched palm connected with nothing. It sliced right through space between the cars, pulling me right down with it.

I went down between the cars so fast, I didn't even realize what had happened. I just knew something strange had occurred because I was now lying on my back, staring up at the underbelly of a giant subway car.

Somehow I had landed vertical along the tracks, missing the electrified third rail entirely. I was instead in the same kind of position you see with people in coffins. Back straight, arms at my sides. But instead of being neatly tucked in ruffles of white satin, I was neatly tucked between the two main rails of the train tracks. Whoa.

"Ryn! Ryn!"

I heard Morty screaming my name, and his arm reaching down for me to grab onto it and get pulled back onto the platform.

"No!" I heard another voice booming. "Don't touch her. Leave her there!"

"Like hell I'm going to leave her there," Morty retorted. I grabbed his hand and he pulled me up.

The booming voice had come from a short, stocky paramedic. She glared at Morty, then at me. She came rambling over and made me sit down on a subway platform bench.

"I'm OK," I said, although I was shaking and lightheaded. Everything felt woozy and surreal, yet I was on a mission to get off the platform to go have a cigarette.

"You are NOT OK," the paramedic screamed in my face. "You'll never be OK. You're going to have nightmares the rest of your life!"

Who IS this woman?

Yeah, OK. I'm really going to sit there and let this lady scream in my face about eternal nightmares. I think not.

I got up, grabbed Morty's arm, and told him we had to get out of there. I was still holding my half-finished beer – which hadn't spilled a drop, by the way. We went down to street level to smoke.

I was still shaking, and everything was blurry. Oh. No wonder it was blurry. I had somehow lost my glasses.

"My glasses! My glasses are gone!" Now I started crying. It turned into wailing.

"We'll get you new glasses," Morty said, giving me a hug.

During the hug, I looked over his shoulder and onto the street, directly beneath the subway tracks. There in a pool of white light were my glasses, with nary a scratch.

"My glasses! My glasses! There they are!"

I picked up my glasses, put them back on my face. We went to the corner deli to get new beers. Then went to call car service to take us into Manhattan to see the Brady Bunch play.

I surely had enough of the subway for one night.

Even though Morty and I had started drinking whenever we felt like it (which was always), we kept our jobs. Or at least he did. One day at the pet shop while I was once again scraping bird poop off the perches, I felt my brain go numb.

Everything had become rather dreary, at least when I wasn't drinking. I hated my job, especially since I had been transferred to the location farthest away from my home.

I had gotten into a hands-on pushing fight with the assistant manager at Larry's shop, a fight that resulted in me getting hurled me into a shelving unit full of aerating fish tank ornaments.

Sure, Mr. Assistant Manager got to stay at Larry's store. I got transferred to uptown Manhattan, a nearly three-hour subway ride from the middle of Brooklyn. Sigh.

If I don't do something, I'm going to end up scraping bird poop off perches for the rest of my life.

I took a break and went to think, grabbing a beer at the corner deli and slamming it as fast as I could.

I know. I'll go to college!

.....LESSONS LEARNEd......

There's a reason there's a yellow line on the subway platform that warns you not to stand too close to the tracks.

God watches out for children, drunks and fools.

Books Before Beer

The same way I thought life would magically be better if I left Michigan for New York, I was certain life would be better if I went to college.

I bet the moment I was able to write "bachelor's degree" on a job application, anyone, anywhere would hire me on the spot. I'd soon be making $9 million dollars a day like Vinnie with his bartender tips.

A new, exciting chapter was about to unfold. I could feel it. I told the pet shop manager to mail my check. I quit.

I went and got an application for Brooklyn College.

My parents came through with the tuition. Since I'd be a full-time student with only a part-time job, they also helped with part of the rent.

My running away had put them through hell on earth for sure, especially since I had not contacted them for a spell after reaching New York. And double especially when they got a call from the cops that a dead body was found that might match their daughter's description.

Obviously, it hadn't been me. But they didn't know that until they got to the morgue.

Their support had always been phenomenal. I was so lucky and grateful they had always been there for me. We were back in touch. They even met – and liked – Morty.

What a wonderful thing they could help me through college. My application was accepted. I'd start in the fall.

A new leaf was turning. Enough of this drinking all day and scraping bird perches.

I would make new rules. No drinking before class. I would get a part-time job where I learned new things. No drinking before work. I would study and buckle down and ace all my classes. A new life. A new me. A new everything!

At the entrance exam, I showed up drunk.

My mom would sometime wonder out loud what heights I could have attained in high school if I had just applied myself. Even just skating through and drinking whenever possible, I had a solid B average, got some honors in something, and won a few journalism awards.

One was for my A to Z review of the Pink Floyd concert. A concert highlight was an inflatable flying pig.

I sometimes do that same wondering, musing what it would have been like if I had not drunk my way through college. Don't get me wrong. I got mostly A's. Two B+. One was for French pronunciation, probably because all my accents end up sounding like an angry Russian.

The other was for a god-awful speech class I was required to take when I fouled up on the speech class screening. The judging panel evidently did not think it was good practice to say "bullshit" when you're up on stage in front of a professional audience.

Despite the haunting B's, I enjoyed the heck out of college. Had the coolest professors. Mastered all the verb tenses and a few swear words in French. Dove into the craft of writing. Studied abroad in England, with two weekends in Paris. Won honors and awards for poetry, writing and even Latin.

All that while getting drunk every single day.

One of those smiling clipboard people came up to me on campus one day. Since the clipboard people are typically poised to yammer on while trying to get you to sign something you don't care about, I was ready to bolt.

But she moved too fast.

"Would you mind taking a survey about drinking?"

What? Finally! Something that interested me.

"Sure."

The survey asked about my grade point average and my drinking habits on a daily and weekly basis. GPA was 3.9 (damn B+).

And let's see. I had six beers yesterday. At least 10 on Monday (damn Mondays).

Oh, and the weekend. That would easily be about 14 to 16 beers per day.

Morty drank about the same rate, now that he was drinking again. We got kicked out of our first apartment some time back for spending all the rent money on Budweiser.

Before I handed the survey back to the smiling girl, I took a quick peek at the survey answers other students gave. GPA 2.2; four drinks over the weekend. GPA 3.1; two drinks on Saturday. GPA 3.6; zero drinking.

Yeah, right. Like someone doesn't drink at all?

The smiling girl took the clipboard, glanced at my answers, and stopped smiling. She now appeared rather confused, even miffed. Maybe she thought I was making light of her survey, or messing it up with a bunch of lies.

If you ask me, it was the students who said they didn't drink at all that were lying. No matter. It was time to go home and crack open my first King of Beers for the day.

I didn't really think Budweiser was the kingliest beer. It was just the cheapest. Or at least the cheapest I would now lower my standards to drink.

Sure, Midnight Dragon malt liquor cost something like 99 cents for a giant bottle that was double the capacity of a single tall boy can of beer. But my Midnight Dragon days were over. I was a college student now. I had at least a bit of class (pun not intended).

For some reason, my undergraduate years galloped by in a blur. I had a routine down pat, one that ensured I did my homework, kept a high GPA, and aced my exams.

Since I had a rule not to drink before class, I made sure all my classes were out of the way as early as possible. Done by noon. Then I'd race home on the Avenue J bus, which actually didn't race at all but rather lumbered and stopped all along the avenue.

Once home, I'd eagerly crack open a beer and start my homework, finishing both as quickly as possible. Once the first beer was popped, it was off to the races. It was a constant race against time.

Would I be able to finish all my homework before I was buzzed enough to not remember anything I had worked on?

Usually, yes. Except I often found scrawled-out, illegible poems on scraps of paper. When I could read them, it was amazing how awful they were.

How did all those drunk writers and musicians get famous if their drunken words and lyrics came out like this?

And studying for a test was a whole different story. That stuff you have to retain for at least an hour or two until you take the exam. Studying while slamming beers the night before wouldn't cut it. So I had to make a change.

I would simply slam beers the night before – then wake up at 3 a.m. to study. It worked! Although it did have a huge drawback once we moved into our second apartment, a dingy dump across from a gas station and above a pizzeria on Brooklyn's Avenue P.

There was a reason why this was pretty much the only apartment for rent we found after we were kicked out of our first apartment. That reason was obvious during my first 3 a.m. study session.

Groggy and discombobulated, I shuffled into the kitchen with my heavy-as-lead chemistry book and flipped on the light. A massive skittering sound filled the air, but I thought it might just be the fog in my brain moving over to get some rote memorization done.

I cracked open the giant, hardcover book to the appropriate chapters, started coming up with fast ways to memorize all this stuff. I pulled out my Sharpie marker and neon index cards to make flashcards.

First term up? Covalent bond.

Plop.

When two atoms share two electrons.

Hmmm....if we think of a double date, that's the two atoms. And the two electrons they share could be two things they have in common.

Plop.

Since it's a double date, they're all in the same car.

Plop. Plop.

And they want to go somewhere fancy that has valet parking.

Plop.

That's it! Double date, shared interests, valet parking. Covalent bond.

Plop. Plip. Plop.

When I turned back to the open chemistry book on the table, what I saw made me jump up and scream.

Every plip and plop that had been going on in the background was the sound of a cockroach falling from the ceiling, smack dab onto the open chemistry book pages.

I had the urge to slam the heavy book shut and crush all the creepy crawly roaches, but I still needed the info in that chapter.

I instead did what any good alcoholic would do at a moment like this. No, I didn't get a drink. It was before class, before a test even! I had my standards.

I did the second-best thing. I shut off the disgust. Pretended it didn't matter. Years of drinking taught me well. I could shut down my emotions in an instant. The wall around my heart was at least 10 miles high and 20 feet thick.

I hadn't cried in years. Even learned how to shut off my ticklish. Move forward. Put on that tough façade. Everything's fine.

Now where were we? Oh yeah, covalent bond.

I got an A on the chemistry test.

Morty and I finally got out of the roachville apartment. But only because we were kicked out after not paying the rent for several months. I sensed a pattern here. Rent, gas, electricity – all those bothersome bills interfered with our beer money.

Once rent time hit, the old man who owned the building would come around and bang on our door. Our loud music and laughter would suddenly stop. We'd quickly shut off the lights.

There. Now he had no idea we're home.

"I know you in there! I know you in there! You told me rent today. Liar man! Liar man! I know you in there, liar man!"

We tried to stifle our laughs while quietly sipping our beers.

The words rang through the hall like a bad Broadway chorus. "Liar man! Liar man! I know you in there, liar man!"

That just made us laugh louder. But we stopped laughing when the old man eventually came by with his son. Morty opened to door to talk with them and the son grabbed and broke Morty's evil eye protection necklace. Then punched Morty in the face.

Jerk.

We made sure to leave several parting gifts for father and son when we moved out. Emptied the entire contents of the fridge into the oven. Ketchup, pickles, mold-ridden vegetable lasagna. Left garbage strewn across the floor. Think we even left our filthy microwave, thanks to what we found beneath it when we moved it.

Colonies of roaches were on the table where the microwave had sat. Upon closer inspection, we saw baby roaches freely teeming in and out of the back of the unit. We poked around in the back with screwdriver. Hundreds of thousands of baby roaches came swirling out, a teeming blanket of disgust.

Guess roaches like electronic stuff. That happened with all the electronics we had in the apartment. We left the worst behind. Literally and figuratively.

Our third and final apartment together was the absolute best. Until it wasn't. It was the place where I finally hit my alcoholic bottom.

⋆·····LESSONS LEARNED······℮

Where there's a will, there's a way. Even if it means waking up at 3 a.m. to study with the roaches.

Never live in an apartment above a pizzeria.

Bottom's Up

But just wait a sec. Not just yet. Drinking your life away will eventually kill you, no doubt. But it's typically a slow and painful death. A very slow and painful death.

Even getting to your bottom can take some time. It all depends on what you consider your bottom to be.

Some people can stop drinking the after their first DUI. Others need to wait until they wake up naked next to a total stranger in a European airport. Others still don't stop until they end up in prison or the psych ward.

The hardest-core alcoholics will take it all the way to the grave.

I had to wait until my body was physically dying, with blood coming out of weird places.

I had given up eating some time back when I realized you could get a quicker beer buzz without the useless food clogging up your stomach. My only nutrients came from Budweiser and the occasional three bites of egg ham cheese potato on a roll from the corner deli.

I had to refuel on beer every 30 minutes or I'd vomit all over the office floor. I'd watch the clock at work, then run outside for a break, thinking I was the sneakiest thing. I'd slam a bottle of Heineken in the phone booth around the corner, thinking I was the sneakiest thing.

The only problem was, around the corner was the busiest street in Sheepshead Bay, Brooklyn. Oh, and the phone booth wasn't a full phone booth. It was one of the one-quarter phone booths that were pretty much a payphone stuck to a pole with a little overhang on top.

By now I was working for a group of Brooklyn community newspapers. I was also into my graduate studies. I finished my Bachelor of Fine Arts in Creative Writing with a French minor and was hyped up with glee to join the full-time workforce.

No I wasn't. The thought of trudging to the same old job day in and day out made me sick to my stomach. Especially since I was still under the impression that the only work that mattered was work that wasn't fun. The only way to make money was with work that wasn't fun. The less creativity involved, the better.

I worked as a part-time bookkeeper during my undergraduate studies. I then asked for an internship as a reporter at the group of local papers. I know! That was fun, so I had to make sure it didn't accidentally turn into a full-time gig.

I didn't want a full-time gig at all, even though I now had a BFA under my belt. Since I had enjoyed my studies so much, and my parents were paying tuition and helping with the rent, why not extend the studies a bit further?

Yes! Let's go get a master's degree!

I applied to the Master of Arts program in English literature at Brooklyn College, then told my parents about my genius plan. It backfired. Sure, they'd help with the tuition. But they were done helping with the rent.

Graduate courses are at night, so I could get a full-time job while going to school, right?

Damn. Sigh. Yes, I guess.

So when an assistant editor opening came up at the newspaper office, I asked if I could trade in my intern reporter status for full-time assistant editor status.

That would work, as editing was far less exciting than reporting. I was at a point where jobs had to be boring for me to feel like it was a real job. And there were a ton of things to edit.

The editorial office churned out nine different community newspapers throughout the week, plus things to mail and things to proof and way too many cooks in the kitchen. If the editorial department found a mistake, it had to go to the design department to ask them to fix it on the final layout.

We then needed a print-out of the final layout of that page to make sure the mistake had been corrected and no new ones were created along the way. I remember being there until after 10 p.m., reading and re-reading pages and pages of tabloid-size proofs.

I also remember running to the bar down the block while waiting for pages to proof.

The flurry of back-and-forth and running across the hall to the design department and then making sure the final printout was really the final one and not the same one as the last one or the one before the last one was a dysfunctional system that inevitably ensured the final product would be pocked with a few mistakes.

The worst one was probably in the front-page story of a hidden subway tunnel that had been discovered under downtown Brooklyn. Whatever organization had sent us the press releasing announcing tours of the tunnel called in a rage, yelling at us as if the front-page typo had been done on purpose.

The mistake was in a sentence talking about how the tunnel, for years, had been sealed shut. The paper had printed that it had been "sealed shit."

★.....LESSONS LEARNED......℮

Never trust a design department that doesn't really like the editorial department.

Fermentation

By now I had a new routine down pat. With classes at night, there was no way I could not drink before class. That's way too long. So I started drinking in the morning. Before work. During work. After work. After class.

Morty and I ordered beer by the caseload from the deli down the block. They delivered. When either of us got paid, our entire checks pretty much went to the deli to pay for the deluge of last week's beer.

The biggest problem here was making sure we ordered the cases early enough so we didn't end up passing out before they showed up with our delivery.

Oh, the tribulations of being a drunk.

And so the cycle continued.

Something smelled foul, and it was us. I'm sure by this point, about 11 years into my daily drinking career, I stank like a walking brewery. There's no way the stench of alcohol could not be oozing from my pores every minute.

Remember Pig Pen from the Peanuts cartoon, how he was surrounded by an aura of filth? I had to be surrounded by an aura of Budweiser. Our cute little third-floor attic apartment also began to stink.

Sure, we did the dishes and all that stuff. Vacuumed and mopped. Morty kind of kept up with the cat's litter box. But it wasn't cat pee that you could smell at the front entrance, three floors down.

It was the smell of yeast. Fermentation. Stale beer.

That's because we had discovered the attic storage area. You could get into it from a little door on the top floor, one of those doors that looks like they were made for fairies or imps.

Behind that door was a big, open space. A space we quickly packed with empty beer cans.

Putting the cans outside in the recycling bin had become ridiculous. They never all fit! We'd put a few in there, the amount the average couple might drink for the week. But that only took care of a dozen or so. That left us with dozens more that had nowhere to go.

That is, until we discovered we could cram them in the crawl space. Then just kind of forget about them and go on with our lives.

Ignoring things had become the name of the game. But the time finally came when I could no longer simply ignore just how bad it had gotten.

In recovery, they're often called moments of clarity. One of my pals refers to them as "epiphanettes." They are those golden moments when you're able to realize and embrace the truth.

Keep in mind, the truth isn't always pretty – but it's always beautiful. Beautiful to no longer have to pretend, deny or be blinded by lies that hold you back.

Like thinking I could actually control my drinking. I had thought that was the case for years. I always told myself I didn't quit drinking because I didn't want to, so there.

"Do you drink every day?" people would ask.

My answer? "I sure as hell try to."

That would usually shut them up. So would another pat answer I was quick to serve up.

"Why do you drink so much?"

"Because I'm an alcoholic. Hahahahahha. Pour me another beer."

I'd constantly joke about being an alcoholic – even though I had no clue what that really meant. I thought it was someone who drank too much and did stupid things. I certainly fit that bill. Ends up most versions of the definition go a tad deeper than that.

It's someone who is addicted to alcohol. Who can't stop drinking once they take that first drink.

In my case, that first drink was now regularly coming at 6 a.m. In fact, the thought of the tall boy Budweiser cans hidden in the vegetable drawer of the fridge was the only thing that got me out of bed in the morning.

Yes, Morty and I were to the point where we were hiding the beer from each other. As if there are so many places to hide tall cans of beer in a fridge that held mustard and a jar of pickles.

Every morning was the same. I would wake up and immediately crack open a beer, sitting and drinking it at the kitchen table the same way people drank their morning coffee. By the third beer I was stable enough to take a shower (with the open beer perched on the side of the tub, of course).

I'd then grab another beer for the subway ride to work, putting it in a little brown bag so I didn't get busted for having an open container on the train.

If I was traveling somewhere and I ran out of beer along the way, I would actually get off at the next subway stop, head out into the street to find a deli to buy another beer (or two), then pay again to get back on the train and continue to my destination.

My workday consisted of sneaking out every 30 minutes to slam a beer. And those things called liquid lunches at the bar down the block.

Before I even sat down at the bar, the bartender would have my three mugs of Budweiser lined up in front of the stool where I usually sat. My lunch break was 30 minutes long, and I could typically slam three big mugs in that amount of time.

I'd pay the bartender, smile and leave. Then one day he said something so cocky I wanted to punch him in the face.

"See you tomorrow," he said with a smile.

See you tomorrow?! See you tomorrow?? Just who does he think he is, telling me where I'll be tomorrow, as if he knows all about me, as if I'm some kind of drunk who will inevitably be back like clockwork.

Holy shit – I am.

That realization was a scary moment, but not as scary as the moment in the office I had turned to respond to whatever my coworker had asked me – and I realized I couldn't speak.

My response was swirling around in my head, but my mouth wouldn't form the words. I ended up babbling some garbled something that made absolutely no sense.

My brain was actually disconnected from my ability to talk.

And then the scariest moment at all. Since my rebellion and drinking started, the big joke in my family was that I would be dead by the time I was 30. Hahahaha. We'd just say it as a matter of fact, yeah whatever, hahahahaha.

But now I was 29 and a half – and rapidly approaching my deathbed.

Even worse, the beer stopped working. No matter how much I drank, I could no longer get drunk. Not even a little buzz. I would drink and drink, end up bloated and sickly. But not as sickly as I'd feel if I didn't drink at all.

And not drinking, I found, was impossible. My whole being had been taken over by a compulsion to crack open and down that beer. I no longer had a choice in the matter. Every waking moment, I obsessed about drinking. Even when I was drinking!

I'd have half a beer left in front of me and be thinking about the next one I was going to drink.

It was hell on earth. The greatest hell. An endless loop of hell. I could no longer get drunk, but couldn't stop drinking.

I can't take this any longer! I can't live like this!

I fell to my knees at the foot of my bed and screamed towards the heavens:

"God please make this stop!"

I woke up the next morning and cracked open a beer.

★.....LESSONS LEARNEd......℮

Few things in life are more horrifying than realizing you're under alcohol's complete control.

Last Call

I asked for help in a roundabout way by accident. God forbid I actually straight-out asked for help – that would be admitting weakness! And I'm strong, capable, independent blah blah and all kinds of other stuff I had been telling myself for years.

But I found myself dialing the number of Cindy, one of my former drinking buddies who had been in recovery for about five years now. She always told me if ever I wanted to quit drinking, just to let her know.

Her husband answered the phone.

"Hey Ryn, how are you?"

"Not good. Not good at all. I'm drinking way too much." It's like a floodgate opened up and I began blathering and crying and wailing in his ear.

"Um…hold on, let me get Cindy."

Cindy and I were to meet at an Alcoholics Anonymous meeting the next afternoon, a Thursday. I prepped by waking up and drinking my usual beers. Then having another beer or two during work breaks until it was time to leave for the 11 a.m. meeting.

I had gotten permission to take a longer lunch. All my coworkers knew where I was going. My drinking through the workday had not been a secret. In fact, they had long encouraged me to stop drinking. I could see the relief on at least two of the faces.

Cindy was waiting for me when I got to the church; the meeting was in the church basement. We walked in to what sounded like happy hour at a bar, but with real happiness instead of drunken guffaws and yelling.

People came up and hugged her. She introduced me, I looked at the floor. Someone asked if I wanted a coffee.

A coffee? A coffee? I hadn't had a coffee in years. I could barely drink water these days without throwing up. How was I supposed to drink a coffee?

"Um, no thank you."

I don't recall much about the meeting except someone in front had a Rod Stewart haircut and the lady leading the meeting said we could talk about anything we wanted.

Oh. And something else. When the lady leading the meeting asked if anyone was there for the first time, I raised my hand and introduced myself. Everyone turned to look at me and say welcome.

I ended up looking into the eyes of the person directly in front of me. Their eyes were warm and happy and alive. It was as if they were welcoming me for real – not just saying it. A comforting feeling immediately shot through my entire body.

It freaked me out. I couldn't wait to leave.

I was even more freaked out by the genuine smiles and laughter that were bouncing around the room. There was no way people could be that jovial, especially without drinking. This had to be some weirdo play act. They had to be pretending.

I **really** couldn't wait to leave. But the next day, I couldn't wait to go back to another meeting. I was drawn to something magical I felt in my soul, even if my brain was busy trying to rebel.

After that first meeting, I never had another drink (knock wood). It was July 22, 1999.

When I got back to work after that first meeting and walked in the office, everyone fell silent and was staring at me. Whoa. I was hit with a flashback of walking into high school that Monday morning after my near-death drinking at the Friday homecoming game.

Instead of staring at me because I went and got drunk, however, now everyone was staring because I went and got sober. Or at least went to a single meeting where someone had a Rod Stewart haircut. Coworkers were bubbling with questions.

"How was it?"

"What did you learn?"

"What did they say?"

"Does this mean you can again come drinking with us at happy hour?"

I had a feeling that's not how it works. I had a feeling I was done drinking forever. The thought was absolutely terrifying, but not as terrifying as the idea of being dead by 30.

I still had way too many things I wanted to do. Dying drunk in 10 months wasn't one of them.

The first week without a drink was excruciating. Mainly because I couldn't stop thinking about a beer. My mind was an endless loop.

Go get a beer. Go drink a beer. How are you supposed to wake up or shower without a beer? How do you take the train without a beer? Get a beer. Drink a beer. Good luck sleeping without a beer!

I made more than one middle-of-the-night phone calls to Cindy, screaming how the obsession would not stop.

"Just don't drink no matter what," she told me. "The cravings will pass. They will. Grab on to the chair if you need to. Just don't drink."

I grabbed onto the chair arms so hard with all my might that my knuckles actually turned white.

Holy moly, another epiphanette. Now I know how they got the term "white knuckling it."

But by day four or so I was getting the hang of sitting through cravings. While they were still maddening, they did start to subside just a bit. Instead of thinking about a beer every single minute, I was only thinking about one every other minute.

I started to feel better physically. I was no longer a 24/7 walking hangover. I could once again brush my teeth without gagging!

Little did I know there was one more horror in store, yet another thing that could have easily killed me. Those creepy things known as the DTs.

*.....LESSONS LEARNED......

Once you quit drinking and then pay off all of your beer tabs, you end up with this strange stuff called money.

AA is not a cult. It's more like a party with people cheering you on to succeed.

Quitting drinking was both the hardest and best thing I have ever done.

Delirium Tremens

Alcoholism is a gift that just keeps on giving. Not only do you get the hell bottom corroded with hopelessness, despair and body so beer-bloated it feels like it's about to pop, but you might also get the delirium tremens.

Delirium tremens refers to a state of extreme alcohol withdrawal when very bad things happen. What kind of bad things? Take a seat, I'll fill you in.

Before we dive down the rabbit-hole of delirium tremens hell, it's important to note two things. The first: The only thing I knew about the DTs was what I saw on a "MASH" episode when I was a kid. It made some guy see worms all over the place.

The second: The DTs certainly couldn't happen to me. I happen to be one of those magical people where things that affect others, like being stood-up on blind dates or losing your wallet, are certainly not going to happen to me.

Besides, based on my deep learning of the DTs based on the "MASH" episode, they only happened to people who drank hard liquor during the Korean War.

Boy was I wrong.

It was at a recovery meeting about five days into sobriety when I noticed the tiles started breathing. They were those ugly green and white tiles you find in old kitchens, and they began to heave up and down.

The ceiling tiles started doing the same. I looked from floor to ceiling, ceiling to floor and both sets of tiles were breathing, breathing, breathing. Then they started rearranging themselves and dancing.

My initial thought was it was kind of cool. It was like an LSD trip but without the risk of losing $20 to a guy with a beat-up red baseball cap.

Maybe sobriety can be fun after all?

While all would have been grand if I saw the tile show and then went home to find everything was back to normal, it wasn't. In fact, I don't remember how I even got home from that meeting at all. And when I walked in the apartment door, it wasn't our apartment.

I mean it was – but it wasn't. It was all rearranged and the bedroom was where the kitchen was supposed to be and the living room was way off to the side, kind of floating. And then everything was upside down.

Yes, I was standing on the ceiling but it was the floor. And somehow the couch was stuck to the ceiling without falling on my head.

I was getting that same feeling you get when you put your shoes on the wrong feet. Or your underwear on inside out and backwards. It was familiar, but wrong.

Then it just got even more wrong.

All the little clay figurines I made all came to life on the shelf, dancing and swirling and jumping up and down. When I tried to sit on the upside-down couch to figure out what was going on, the cushions broke open and worms were squirming inside.

Damn "MASH" episode!

Things moved from fun to terrifying in an instant.

Because I knew we were not alone. Morty and I were not the only people in the house. I saw a whole Mexican family living under the coffee table.

They were hanging out, somehow all fitting under there just fine, smiling and laughing like it was natural to live under a coffee table in an upside-down, third-floor Bensonhurst attic apartment.

The family of four wasn't the only one keeping an eye on what was going on. It was then I realized there were tape recorders and microphones in all the heating vents. And people on the other side of the wall, listening.

I remember whispering, telling Morty not to speak too loudly or they'll hear. He looked at me, confused, turning back to the TV. But they were in the TV, too!

I sat down at my word processer to type up everything that was going on so I'd have a record of all this spying. That, and to type a secret note to Morty since he apparently didn't get that we were being watched and recorded.

He even pretended not to see the whole family under the coffee table!

As I was typing up a litany of the horror, I suddenly realized they were in the word processor, too! I couldn't type anything they could use against me. I couldn't let them know I knew they were watching and listening.

I had to act like I wasn't on to them. Work on something else instead. So I decided it would be a good time to add a chapter or two to my master's thesis, a two-year research project on the folklore of New York City subway workers. It was in its final stages.

Yeah, now would be a great time to work on my thesis.

But the gnats made it impossible to concentrate. It started with a few random gnats on my word processor screen. But then more and more came until a whole swarm of them were dancing around my head. Buzzing and dancing and buzzing and flitting, and damn I had to get away from them.

So I jumped in the shower. I don't recall if I had bothered to take my clothes off, but I do recall having one of the most frightful thoughts I ever had in my entire life: I am losing my mind!

I had always wondered if crazy people knew they were crazy. Now I was seeing firsthand how, at least at first, they probably knew the crazy was happening. I felt my mind cleave in half, with the sane part slipping away, like the key that falls under a car, just out of reach.

I kept reaching and reaching for it, trying to reel it back, but it was floating away. All rational thoughts and logic were somehow disconnecting from my brain, leaving me reeling in a pit of madness.

It was then I was suddenly being chased by the devil, his wife, and a squatty Mexican man with a gun. The devil just so happened to look like a former boss. His wife still looked like his wife.

And I had no idea why or how this Mexican man came into the picture. Maybe he was somehow connected to the family under the coffee table?

Being chased in a 500-square-foot attic apartment doesn't leave you much room to run. Or hide. Especially when the squatty man kept appearing in weird places, just when I had thought I outwitted him. He even came up the dumbwaiter that had suddenly appeared in our kitchen cupboard.

I had to get out. I had to get away! So I began to open the third-floor window to jump out and flee this danger. Morty sprang into action, tackling me and holding me down so I couldn't jump.

He quit drinking a day before I did. Although he wasn't hit with the DTs, he was going through his own withdrawal symptoms. One was constant puking, including puking all over the living room carpet as he held me down to save my life.

Wrassling. Tackling. Puking. Screaming. Crying. Kicking. Wailing in terror.

And the DTs weren't done yet.

I managed to slip out of Morty's grip and lock myself in the bedroom. I grabbed the phone and called 911, reporting the two gunmen and one gun woman who were trying to kill me, and how one got loose through the dumbwaiter.

Flashlights were soon all over the yard as cops scoured the area around the house. Landlord came upstairs, wanting to know what was going on. Two officers came up, telling us they didn't find anyone with guns in the yard.

They checked the kitchen cabinet. The dumbwaiter had somehow mysteriously disappeared. The landlord said there had never been one, ever.

A moment of clarity hit. I needed help. Morty gave the police and landlord a rundown on how we just quit drinking and what was going on.

"Take me to the hospital," I said.

Police called an ambulance. Another moment of clarity hit in the ambulance when I heard the medics talking about the hospital known for housing crazy people and being haunted.

"Let's take her to Bellevue," they said.

"NO!" I sat up from the gurney like a shot. "Take me to Maimonides."

They changed course to Maimonides Hospital in Brooklyn as I slithered back onto the gurney and into the pit of madness.

It was then I saw the pizza delivery van. The gunmen and woman were still after me, following the ambulance in a pizza van!

"Faster, faster," I screamed, "drive faster! They're catching up."

"Um, I don't even see a pizza delivery van."

"It's there. It's there!"

They sped up anyway.

The next part of the DTs was a whirlwind of checking in to the hospital, being admonished by the nurse for quitting cold turkey, seizures that made my eyeballs roll back into my head, and lots of IV fluids.

I vaguely recall begging for police protection of my hospital room to save me from the killers in the pizza delivery van.

I woke up what seemed like three lifetimes later, with a woman police officer standing over my hospital bed.

"I had a friend who quit drinking and went through the same thing," she told me. "You're going to be fine."

I was suddenly blanketed in a soothing sense of peace and love. I was going to be fine. The police woman said so. I drifted off to sleep.

When I woke up, the police woman was gone. I asked around to find out where she went. I wanted to thank her. But there had been no police woman on duty who came to the hospital that night. In fact, no one remembers seeing her at all.

I know she wasn't a hallucination. I was done with them by then. I remain convinced she was an angel. Just one of the many who had helped save my life and soothe my soul during the umpteen times I should have been dead.

*.....LESSONS LEARNED......

If I never drink again, I'll never have to go through the DTs again.

I NEVER want to go through the DTs again.

Part 2
Sea Legs

God, please grant me
Direction to choose that path
Determination to stay on that road
Strength to continue that journey
And a jaunt to do it in style.

-Ryn Gargulinski, 1999

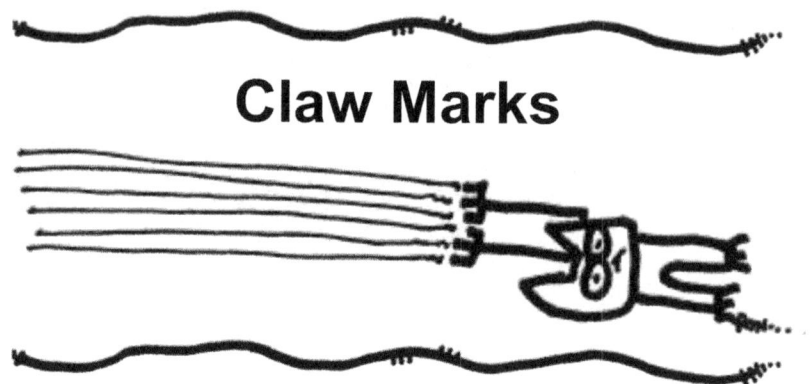

Claw Marks

The alcohol and DTs were out of my system. But I still needed to get one more thing out of my system. That thing was Morty.

Yes, we were in love at one time, and perhaps it's one of those loves that lasts forever. But our relationship had been long gone, drowned in a sea of beer. And as I started to blossom and grow in my recovery, he stayed the same.

He wasn't drinking any longer. At least not beer.

Instead of sitting around watching TV in the middle of the cramped apartment living room slamming beers, he sat around watching TV in the middle of the cramped apartment living room slamming water.

I was into the water-slamming, too. It was as if our bodies had turned into automated puppets that needed to keep performing the hand-to-mouth motion of drinking a beer.

Put anything there. A cigarette. A cupcake. Water. We still drank and drank for hours on end.

Morty actually drank so much water that he ended up in the emergency room. All that water was flushing the electrolytes from his system. How do you like that? You quit drinking just to end up in the hospital anyway. Again, with something that could take his life.

It wasn't the first time a doctor warned him he would die if he didn't stop his excessive drinking. But this time he needed to stop excessively drinking water.

Sigh. That wasn't the only thing that needed to change. As I started going to AA meetings, I started to see how bad my life really had become. I figured I would stop drinking and everything would turn into some kind of rainbow-and-peonies world.

But it was still a small, dark place that held the residual smell of beer cans and a cat box that needed to be changed.

That described the apartment – as well as my mind.

I went to more AA meetings. They always made me feel better, even back when I had a brief glimpse of them around age 16. Attending AA meetings had been part of my probation after I tried to steal a pint of Southern Comfort from a Midwest superstore.

Attending AA meetings had probably been the highlight of my probation, much more fun than the monthly visits with the probation officer. And definitely more fun than the community service, which involved wearing a bright orange vest and picking up garbage in the park.

I went to the meetings as required, enjoying lots of laughter and crazy stories.

There were plenty of solutions offered, too, but I had not been ready to hear them. I had taken absolutely none of it seriously. I had been a 16-year-old kid merrily playing with fire.

But now I was a 29-year-old woman who was burnt to the core of my soul. It was no longer fun and games. It had become life or death.

I only turned to AA because I didn't want to die.

Even though I initially didn't want anything to do with the 12 steps, I did get a sponsor. I also made it my mission to go to a meeting every single day – even if I was still pretty skeptical.

I met people who said they'd been sober for months. Years. Decades! I was sure they were lying. Just as I was sure their laughter wasn't genuine, their hugs weren't heartfelt, and their joy wasn't real.

Then one day I got a glimpse. I don't remember when it happened, where I was or what I was doing at the time, but I remember a burst of light came into my heart. For a split second or so, I was infused with the most energetic, beautiful essence. I thought I was dying. I called my sponsor. It wasn't death at all.

It was joy.

Whew. Kind of like vanilla coffee or really good Chinese food, once you get even the smallest taste of it – you need more and more. Or at least I did.

I needed more joy. I wanted it now! Man oh man, I needed more of that brilliant, bright feeling.

How do I get it? How can I keep it? How can I have it every minute, every day?

Then the really bad news came down the pike.

To feel like that always, you need to do the work.

Dammit. Dammit. Dammit.

Now more and more dammits were all I felt more of. Particularly because I knew "the work" consisted of those scary-looking 12 steps on a big white poster in the front of the room in the AA recovery meetings.

Big black letters on a stark white background mentioned creepy words like "powerlessness," "amends," and another one that REALLY gave me the heebie-jeebies: "God."

The God word really struck a chord because of everything I had associated with it in the past. I thought you could only communicate with God through priests and bishops and that guy who rode around in a Pope Mobile.

In fact, God only cared about priests and nuns and Pope Mobile passengers. He surely didn't have the time or energy to care about someone like me.

God made me think of getting grounded for not going to church. Or sitting through stuffy boring masses, craving a cigarette.

Or that weekend I spent the night at Grandma P's house and told her I was too sick to go to church on Sunday morning.

"OK fine," she said, heading off on her own.

Whoa, I just got away with murder! No way did Grandma P, this woman who sent her kids to Catholic school and went to church several times a week, just let me off the hook.

I thought I was quite a crafty kid.

Until she came home, plopped me in front of the TV, and turned on a station that aired mass after mass for 24 hours on Sundays – and made me watch it all day long.

Yeah, up until this point in my life, God to me was a pain in the ass.

Living the way I was living became a pain in the ass, too. That's because I wasn't really living. I was merely surviving. Still scraping by from one day to the next. Not necessarily money wise – we were suddenly rich once we paid off all our beer debts at the deli and didn't have to spend hundreds a week on more beer.

I felt better physically, but my mind and soul still felt like they were beat up and lying in the gutter.

The steps creeped me out, so I avoided them at all costs. But the recovery meetings felt great. It was so beautiful – yet absurd – to be in a room full of people who knew exactly how I felt. I don't think that had EVER happened in my life.

And if it did, I would have probably never known it. Because I rarely told the truth about how I really felt. This was most obvious at the end of my drinking, when I was essentially a walking hangover. Headache. Body ache. Nausea. Scrambled egg for brains.

Every morning I used to tell myself: No one has to know how you really feel. No one has to know how you really feel.

Now I not only told the truth about how I felt, but people actually related it to it. Whoa is right. For the first time in my life, I felt like I truly belonged.

I hated to say it at the time, but those recovery people were right. They had told me that my relationship with Morty was not destined to last if I began to change and he didn't.

Within my first year of sobriety, I got a new job, got a new haircut. I instantly lost all the beer bloat, making me appear slimmer and healthier. Creativity that had been stifled for years came out in a massive gush. That first year of recovery, I wrote more than 1,000 poems.

Morty sat on the couch, sipping water and watching TV.

I took up yoga and meditation. Started going to the gym and poetry readings. Bought a brand-new bicycle.

Morty sat on the couch, sipping water and watching TV.

I finally acquiesced. As much as the steps creeped me out, I was told they were the key to feeling better. Fine. I started working through them.

Morty sat on the couch, sipping water and watching TV.

All the changes were pretty thrilling. Especially the part about losing the beer bloat. But the idea of changing the situation with Morty was downright terrifying.

Even though our relationship had petered out some time back, living together was all I had known for the past decade. Living on my own without Morty was a great unknown. Actually, when I looked back at it, living on my own, period, was a great unknown.

In my head I was this fiercely independent rebel who didn't need anything from anybody, thank you very much. But in reality, it was a different story.

I went from living with my parents to living with Jax and crew. Then living with Big John. Then living alone, but with Vinnie paying my rent. Then living with boss and his fiancé. Then living with Morty.

Oh man, I had NEVER lived alone. No wonder I was so dang scared by the idea of moving out.

It was also a huge step to admit the relationship was over. We knew it was over in our hearts, sure. But to admit it out loud – or actually make it official by moving out – was a whole different thing.

Oh, all this thinking made my head hurt. So I stayed living with Morty for another two years.

*.....LESSONS LEARNED......

Fear is a great paralyzer. It's really good at keep you stuck, making you think the misery you know is preferable to anything you don't know. So you'll never know if what's waiting is bliss.

Going Solo

"And the day came when the risk to remain tight in a bud was more painful than the risk it took to blossom." - Anais Nin

The day finally came. I was moving out.

The decision hit home during my usual morning meditation. Not because some glorious, larger-than-Texas angel descended and told me what to do (I'm still waiting for that). But because I realized I was crumpled up in the dark, sitting cross-legged on peeling yellow-gold linoleum, under the kitchen table next to a smelly cat box.

That was actually my usual meditation spot. Some book I read said to find a secret corner where I could have peace, quiet and solitude. The only corner not stuffed with stuff was here under the kitchen table. No one in their right mind would be coming 'round this area.

I guess I never realized how grotesque it was to meditate inhaling the smell of cat pee with pebbles of strewn litter sticking to my thighs. Not until that day.

A giant lightbulb went off in my head.

What a bunch of hooey! That's it. I'm outta here.

My first solo apartment, ever. Wow. It had a cozy back bedroom with hardwood floors, a single closet, and white living room carpet (which I thought was the strangest color to pick for a New York City anything).

And no more peeling yellow-gold linoleum in the kitchen. This one had peeling drab whitish linoleum instead.

Moving out was scary and hard. Really hard. Especially since Morty refused to help in any way. I had to recruit my then-sponsor to help me pack and move the one and a half piece of furniture that was mine. That would be a 1970s end table and cork lamp, courtesy of Grandma G.

Nothing was bothering me on the day that it finally sank in – I was a blissfully single woman living on my own in New York City. Wooohoooo!

No more answering to anyone. No more listening to the TV drone from the middle of the living room. No more meditating next to a cat box.

The realization hit while I was on my bicycle, zooming down New Utrecht Avenue in the middle of Brooklyn, under the elevated subway train.

The Who song started running through my head: "I'm FREE – I'm free!" Those were the only words I remembered, but the music was going and going, filling me with the greatest elation.

I was on a side street now, zooming and zigging and zagging on my bike. I made a sharp, diagonal cut near an intersection to get back to New Utrecht. It was a quick detour that put me in the lane of oncoming traffic. No traffic was coming, so I was good.

Until a car appeared out of nowhere, making a left turn right into me. I looked to my left: the car. I looked to my right: a curb full of garbage cans. Shit.

I closed my eyes and braced for impact.

When I opened my eyes, I was still on my bicycle, pedaling away, now riding blithely down New Utrecht as if nothing had happened. The car was now behind me, the driver's head sticking out the window, looking in my direction with his mouth agape.

The trash cans were still upright on the curb. I was actually in the proper bike lane. I had not hit a single thing. It took me a minute to make sure I really wasn't dead. Then I rode the rest of the way home, The Who song in my head replaced by a colossal wave of gratitude in my heart.

Thank you. Thank you. Thank you.

Dang. There certainly IS a God. And he DID care about me. All I had to do to believe that one was count up the dozens of times I should have been dead.

Including the time I almost married a psychopath.

✱.....*LESSONS LEARNED*.....℮

There's an angel for everything. Including reckless biking on New Utrecht Avenue.

The Psychopath

"He's not a boy. He's a man! You're dating a man!" That was one coworker's glowing review of Johann, after she saw us kissing during a lunch break while waiting to cross Madison Avenue.

Neatly pressed suit. Full-time manager-level office job. Expensive-looking watch. Tassel shoes. That was Johann. I guess that was all man-like, although I could certainly do without the tassel shoes.

Johann and I met through mutual acquaintances in recovery. It was around Valentine's Day, and he started the wooing immediately. A giant teddy bear. A box of chocolates. A flourishing bouquet of roses sent to my workplace. I never had anyone woo me like that. I guess that's what men do?

I fell fast and hard.

After dating a couple of weeks, he wanted me to move in with him. Wow. The idea tickled my spine, but there was no way I was giving up my Brooklyn apartment. That, and he lived in Queens.

It had taken a lot of kicking and screaming to get me to move from Manhattan to Brooklyn. And now I loved Brooklyn. Queens? I think not.

So we did the next best thing. He would stay at my place. I would stay at his place. He would buy me jewelry and things. I would swoon and thank him. After another few weeks, he asked me to marry him.

My gut fluttered with excitement. Wow. I immediately started envisioning a happily-ever-after life with this bona fide MAN.

We could get a really cool place together. We'd do weekend getaways in that upstate New York cabin he kept mentioning. We'd sing, laugh and dance, cook each other stir-fry.

Oh, how badly I wanted to be in love! Who cared if I didn't really know him. I wanted this life of love.

"OK, yeah, sure. I'll marry you."

He took me to a jewelry shop, told me to pick out anything I wanted. I went for a white-gold blue sapphire and diamond ring that had to be custom made. Of course. If I can pick anything, I'm going to pick the best. He put down the nonrefundable deposit.

We sang, we laughed, we danced all the way home.

But the singing, laughing and dancing didn't last all that long. The more time we spent together, the more I realized that fluttering gut may not have been excitement. It may have been a big block of fear, telling me to run.

We spent less time at my place, more time at his. His rented house in Queens required a car ride to the bus station to get to the subway train. He needed to know where I was every minute of the day. He would listen in on the phone calls to my mother. Told me my friends didn't love me as much as he did.

The one time he allowed me to cook stir-fry at his house, he stood behind me with a broom to sweep up anything I dropped before it even hit the floor.

His suits were neatly pressed, sure. And so were his ties and shirts. This man even ironed and hung up his blue jeans.

One morning I went for my usual weekend walk, but it was before he woke up. About 20 minutes into my refreshing stretch of freedom, I saw he was tailing me down the Queens street in his giant red truck.

My stomach dropped into my toes.

Great. I can't get away from this guy for two seconds!

I tried to rationalize why he'd come prowling the streets looking for me.

Maybe he just cared a lot? Maybe he wanted to surprise me?

I kept talking myself into the beauty of love, ignoring the churning in my gut and the tension in my head. Maybe a weekend trip to that luxury cabin he kept mentioning would help things get better.

The cabin ended up being a leaky trailer in the woods. It was infested with ants and reeked of mold and mothballs.

I wanted to puke.

I made a feeble attempt at trying to break things off after the leaky-trailer weekend. Yuck. Man or not, if Johann refers to his broken-down trailer as a luxury cabin, I'd hate to know what other delusions he's feeding me.

I told him I needed some breathing space. He showed up at my apartment the next night.

Once again, I was blinded by the desire to be in love. I let him in.

I played the game a little longer, letting him buy me things and pretending everything was A-OK. He became more and more controlling, insisting I attend all the same recovery meetings as he did. Waiting outside my workplace building during lunch breaks. Calling my desk every 20 minutes or so, just to make sure I'd answer.

He'd admonish me for not wearing the jewelry he bought me, which included a giant, sparkly elephant pendant that was as close to my style as a pink hair bow.

He once yelled at me for chatting with a dude after one of our recovery meetings, even punched his truck door to punctuate his anger.

Look what I made him do, Johann told me. That's how much he loved me. Couldn't I see?

From an outside perspective, the next move is obvious. Leave the jerk and move on with your life. But when you're inside an abusive relationship, things are far less cut and dry.

There are all kinds of emotions involved, especially fear. Trying to leave the dude may be the deadliest move you ever try to make. Worse than falling under a moving subway train.

I also had to deal with feeling like a total idiot.

How did I let him get so close to me, so fast? Why didn't I see this coming?

It was somehow my fault all this was happening. If I broke it off, it would underscore how stupid and wrong I had been for dating this guy.

I didn't want to be stupid and wrong. It was easier to just stay with him than deal with this bastion of emotions and shame. It was easier to stay and hope he'd change – or maybe even drop dead.

It finally got to the point where I couldn't merely sit around hoping any longer. I snapped.

Enough is enough of this bullshit! I can't live like a specimen in a jar. I don't even love this man. He's trying to control my every move. Get him away from me.

I exploded with anger and disgust – in the privacy of my bathroom. But I had an inkling not to confront Johann with the same level of emotion.

After all, he did brag about how he could silently kill a deer in the distance with the crossbow he kept under his bed. "No one would ever know." He then showed me the crossbow.

And once stopped at a red light in his big red truck, he said how he'd mow over his ex-wife if she happened to be crossing in front of him.

No, I had to be gentle with this breakup. Better do it in a semi-pubic place, too, so he doesn't run to get the crossbow. I chose the end of my lunch break, as he was walking me back to my office building.

I took a deep breath. Looked at my shoes for inspiration. "Umm… I don't think it's working out."

"Just give me another chance. I'm sorry!"

"Umm…nah, well, I think we need to, you know, break up."

"But I love you! I need you! I put a nonrefundable deposit on that ring!"

"Sorry…but it's over."

I scurried into the office building like a scampering rat, made a beeline across the marble lobby to the elevator bank. Pushed and pushed and pushed the UP button. When is this dang thing going to come?!

Behind me I heard his screams echoing through the lobby.

"You fucking bitch! You worthless piece of shit! You can't do this to me. You can't DO this to me! To me! To ME!!!!"

The elevator finally came. I got up to my desk, crying and shaking. Explained what happened to the coworker who had called Johann a man. She now called lobby security to tell them never to let a man named Johann Blahblah past the front desk. We'd bring down a photo of him in a minute.

My desk phone rang. It was Johann.

"I'm sorry," he said. "I didn't mean it. Will you please give me another chance?"

I hung up the phone without saying a word.

Thus began his reign of terror.

Johann began calling me at all hours of the day and night – on my cellphone, my home phone, at work – at work, on my cell, on my cell – at home, on my cell, at work at home at work at home on my cell on my cell.

The phone would not stop ringing. It was Chinese water torture, but a hell of a lot louder. And longer.

He left what felt like 837 messages. Message after message after message. They went from pissed off to apologetic to downright begging.

"Please, please, give me another chance."

I thought the begging was bad until he started threatening to kill himself if we didn't reunite. When that didn't work, he started threatening to kill me.

He screamed. He whispered. He ranted. The guy went psycho. In a nutshell, he went nuts.

Here's where I had two choices – live with the terror in the pit of my stomach, the one that felt like a blender full of beets on purée – or go to the cops.

Based on all the true crime I've watched and read, I knew the cops would be a tough sell. But I went to the nearest Brooklyn precinct anyway. I brought my friend Margie for support.

The officer took my report, listened to a handful of the 837 messages I'd been clever enough to record.

"He never outright says he's going to kill you," she said.

Apparently, "I'll chop you up and throw you in the Dumpster where you belong" didn't count as a death threat.

I was about to slink off with my tail between my legs. Figured I'd book a one-way ticket to some obscure island with a name I couldn't pronounce where he'll never find me.

But Margie was not about to slink anywhere. She instead stood up, looked the police officer in the eye, and demanded: "What kind of evidence to you need – a dead body? We're not going anywhere until we get some help."

She plopped back down on the seat with a glare slicing through the officer.

I was immediately assigned two excellent Brooklyn detectives. They became my new best friends. They listened to me. They believed. They were actually as concerned as I was about the throw-you-in-the-Dumpster message.

I got an order of protection.

The detectives gave me helpful hints, all of which I followed like they were going to be on a test. I guess they were. A test for my life.

They escorted me home and give my apartment a safety check. Oh, and the big one.

They threw Johann in a jail. While they couldn't get Johann for killing me or violating the order of protection (yet), they could get him for the 837 nasty phone calls.

Aggravated harassment is a crime. They had his address, said they'd pick him up in the middle of the night, wake him up at like two in the morning.

I kept picturing Johann being dragged from his bed in his baggy boxer shorts and wife beater tank top, then being thrown, slumped all sleepy, in a jail cell.

Yessssssss. I was planning to do anything I could to make him pay.

Then I just wanted to forget. To move on.

But forgetting and moving on would be a tough one since he still had a ton my possessions at his Queens house. Including a $1,500 laptop.

No way was I going to pay a visit to go get them. The cops had no proof any of the stuff was mine.

It felt like my insides were gutted. I was also angry at myself for ignoring the whole lineup of warning signs.

Like the fact he wanted to spend every sleeping and waking moment together into the next life – even if I came back as a goat. Or the fact that he'd get upset if I made phone calls on my cell phone when I was at his house, instead of using his home phone landline (remember those?).

Or the time he was befuddled when I didn't want to come watch him wash his car one Saturday morning. Or miffed when I wanted to spend time walking, biking or with friends. Or downright livid when I said we should maybe spend an occasional Sunday apart.

The final straw should have been the dog-sitting incident, when the dog he was watching wouldn't stop barking. Putting the dog out in his truck for the night only made the neighbors call the cops to report the incessant barking.

He brought the dog inside, and it was finally quiet. The next morning, I found the dog in the closet with his muzzle duct-taped shut, standing next to a pile of his own feces.

I was done pretending this was love. This was something caustic and detrimental. And I wanted out. Now.

And boy, did it hurt. As much as love zoomed me to the stratosphere as a soaring bird, the twisting thereof plummeted me into the horrid depths of hell, especially when a person I had trusted with my life now seemed to want to get rid of it.

As tough as it was to move past this one, I wouldn't let it get me down. I promised myself I would emerge victorious. Scalded with hell-burnt bald spots, but victorious nonetheless.

I will never again shut the door on my instincts. I will never again jump too fast into a relationship. I won't shun my own needs and my friends. And I will never again automatically trust someone just because they give me a teddy bear.

I will not, I will not, I won't!

At least until the next time.

★.....LESSONS LEARNEd......℮

Control freaks take over slowly, stripping away pieces of your identity and sanity bit by bit. Before you know it, you're in their clutches – wondering what the heck happened. Escape is not as easy as it may seem.

Don't date dudes who keep crossbows under their bed.

Why Bother?

Keeping my promise to myself to stay away from relationships was easy at first. I was way too busy doing other things. Like writhing on the bedroom floor in the most godawful agony, wanting to die.

Recovery may have made me all bright-eyed and bushy tailed on the outside, but there was a dark part of me that was still lurking inside. A real dark part.

Dark enough to bring on crazy thoughts. Sometimes I'd be sitting and chatting with someone, someone I liked even, and I'd suddenly envision bashing them on the back of the head with a cast iron skillet.

Other times, if I stared too hard at someone, their eyes would start melding into one big eye, and then their whole face would start to melt.

No, it wasn't residual alcohol or hallucinogens. By now I had not touched a drink or drug for at least five years. And this was not the same kind of feeling drinking or drugs would typically deliver.

I didn't know what it was. And it scared the hell out of me. Especially since it would randomly come and go, disrupting any given day at any given moment.

There were times I would be in the middle of my run-of-the-mill routine and a giant thought would pop into my head:

This is absurd. This is ALL absurd! Life is absurd! What they heck are we doing here? Why do we even bother?

By now I had found massive relief with the recovery habits I wove into my daily life, but this weirdness was kind of putting a damper on that thing called inner peace.

After all, it is tough to float around in a cloud of serenity when you're bombarded by random thoughts of smashing a cast iron skillet into the back of someone's skull.

I shared about it at recovery meetings. I started to hate going to recovery meetings. I started to hate the people AT the recovery meetings. I started to hate all the people everywhere.

The weirdness and pain kept getting greater and greater. I thought continuing to go to recovery meetings would at least help ensure I didn't go drink over this horrible thing. And maybe even give me some relief.

It did help me not drink. But it didn't really bring relief. In fact, a comment from one of the meeting attendees made things five dozen times worse.

I had been sharing honestly, because we're taught to be honest. Well, I did leave out the bit about bashing in skulls with a frying pan.

I shared of the dark cloud of horrible thoughts and how life would suddenly become absurd and how I hated everybody and everything and yes, even you.

One woman said, "It's OK. We love you anyway. You'll get through this. You're in the right place."

Another woman said, "It's because you're not working your program hard enough."

Never mind the beautiful words of encouragement from woman number one. I instead grabbed onto the comment from the second woman and ran. Ran all the way home.

What am I doing wrong? How can I be doing it WRONG??!! Why aren't I getting it!

Don't forget, I managed to maintain a 3.9 GPA in college while trying to drink myself to death.

How could I be doing something wrong now, now that I was clear-headed and sober?

This made no sense. None of it made sense. It may have been that day or the next day or a week down the line but one afternoon I found myself writhing on my bedroom floor.

I was howling in anguish. Absolutely HOWLING.

There was nothing in my outer life that would have created so much pain. Something was exploding on the inside.

Something that shot tendrils of agony through my entire being. Just when I thought I could take no more, a big, booming voice echoed through my head:

"What if. There is. NO GOD."

"Noooooorrrrrggghhhhhhhhaaaaaaaanoooooooooooooooooooooo!" A horrified yowl erupted from my soul. My body, mind and spirit turned inside out in a split second, my exposed insides shaking with sheer terror.

For a millisecond, my worst nightmare had come true. That there was no God, there was no afterlife, there was no heaven. We were just little useless drones marching onward in our little useless lives only to eventually drop dead and turn into NOTHING!

I wouldn't be me. I would be nothing. I would be nothing. Nothing. Nothing, like I never even existed.

This ghastly thought had haunted me my entire life. I remember waking up in the middle of the night screaming as kid, maybe not out loud, but into my pillow. I remember trying to stuff the thought away as an adult. Stuff it away as quickly as it came.

Drinking it away had been my main course of action. But at that very minute I did not want to drink. And if there's no God, heaven or afterlife, I certainly didn't want to die. Or maybe I should, and just get it over with…make this agony GO AWAY.

I'd rather be NOTHING than live with THIS PAIN.

I laid there and prayed. Laid and prayed. Laid and prayed and prayed until I finally fell asleep.

Age 35. That's how old I was before I was FINALLY, blissfully diagnosed with depression. I say blissfully because it was such a relief to have an explanation for the heaviness in my heart. The black spot in my soul. The craziness in my head.

It's so much easier to find a solution when you understand what you're dealing with. And so much easier for therapists to help you figure out what you're dealing with when you actually tell them the truth.

I had been dragged into therapy for years, starting when I was a kid. I had lied to them all. No, wait! I recall once telling the truth. It had been in response to that all-time annoying go-to question when there's a lull in the conversation and the therapist has no idea what else to say.

"How do you feel?"

"I feel like punching you in the face."

There it was. The one time I was truthful. I think the session ended shortly thereafter.

My response must have come during my surly teen years, although I recall a rage deep inside me that had started much earlier than that. Uncontrollable tantrums. Screaming and kicking.

Any concerned parent would try to do something for a child that was in so much anguish. So mine did. And the merry-go-round began. I'd lie to the therapist. They'd have no clue what was going on or what to do for me. We'd go home, I'd be good for a while.

Then the snarling red rage would rear its horrific head. I'd break something valuable. Back into therapy we'd go.

During one intro session with a new doc, I was told to go wait in another room instead of going back to my parents after the session. The next thing I knew, some orderlies were taking my shoelaces away.

Yep. I got admitted to some psychiatric facility for angry teens. I don't remember what I said in the intro session with that guy. But I guess it was something I shouldn't have.

I spent a few weeks there. Ate only cottage cheese in protest. Turned into some kind of role model by accident. By the end of my stint at "the asylum" as I called it, the only thing all the teen girl patients would eat was – you guessed it – cottage cheese.

Even the asylum couldn't figure out all that rage was actually depression. Depression turned inside out, masquerading as anger. Anger was familiar to me. It made me feel powerful. I had learned to turn pretty much every emotion into anger.

That tough chick I pretended to be? You're not going to see her cry. Ever.

All grief, sadness and despair? Turn it into anger. Those feelings of being excluded, an outcast, scared and ashamed? Turn them into anger. Turn them into anger. An anger so potent that it made me totally lose control.

An anger so deep, it wanted to kill me. And I'm sure it would have. Had I not found alcohol.

Alcohol turned everything off. Let me slip into a total oblivion. Drinking for me was never fun. It was a way to stay alive.

But here we were, years later, with drinking no longer an option. Seemed being honest was the only choice. Besides, the therapy sessions were coming out of my paycheck now, not my parents. I'm not about to spend some $75 an hour (with insurance) just to sit around and lie to the person I'm paying.

When it comes to depression, I've learned there are dozens of things to try before you get to the "evil" M-word. Medication. I thought medication was evil because I viewed it as a sign of weakness. Like that one woman said at the recovery meeting, it was a sign I just wasn't "working my program" hard enough.

Never mind I had embraced the life of recovery, and everything that came with it. Things like eating healthy. Exercise. Getting enough sleep. Connecting with people who cared. Prayer. Meditation. You name it, I was doing it.

And never mind, too, that the Big Book of Alcoholics Anonymous (the most helpful recovery book I ever met) said seeking outside help from professionals beyond the recovery circle was sometimes necessary. I shared my fears with friends and acquaintances – found out some had been taking antidepressants for years and I didn't even know it!

Well, OK fine. I guess the chemical imbalance found in my brain is something that needs a bit more help than eating spinach every day. The therapist sent me to a psychiatrist for a prescription. Because everyone is unique, it can several attempts to find a medication that works.

We got one that worked on the first try.

See? There is a God. Take that, stupid booming voice in my head.

For the record, I never heard that horrible booming voice again. I even stopped imagining bashing people in the back of a head with a cast iron skillet. Or at least people I liked.

....Lessons Learned......

Depression is nothing to be ashamed of. Neither is seeking help to treat it. Sure beats the bejesus out of writhing in agony on the floor.

The God Thing

The God thing had stopped freaking me out when I learned a secret trick in recovery. You don't have to stay stuck with the God you were taught or the God you constructed after years of being grounded for not going to church.

You could make up your own God.

What?! You mean a God I can talk to directly, without the help of priests or priest assistants when the priest is out of town? A God who actually cares about you, even if you're not a nun?

A God that's not an angry old man on a mountain, waiting to strike you down the first time you tell an authority figure to blow it out their ass? (If that would have been the case, I would have been struck down about 100 times over.)

The very thought of it felt like blasphemy. I was sure I would be hit by lightning or swallowed whole by a New Utrecht pothole for toying with this radical idea that I could make up my own version of God.

But I wasn't. Making a version of God was tougher than I thought it would be. Felt nearly impossible to shake all those previous beliefs. Someone told me to jumpstart the process by making a list of traits my God had.

Ummm... Let's see.

I racked my brain, thinking of traits a God that was friends with me would have. For months, there were only two traits on the list. My God had a sense of humor. And he liked tattoos.

As I grew, my God grew. He started gaining traits left and right. He was kind. Caring. Compassionate. Hilarious.

I liked him so much, I started imagining he was riding on the subway next to me, coming along wherever I went. (If you ever want to keep an empty seat next to you on the subway, just tell people God is already sitting there.)

I started having a lot of fun with this God concept. Even drew a cartoon of what my God would look like. It was a little blue stick-figure-looking man I called Boobala God.

I showed the drawing to my new then-sponsor, who immediately said there was a problem with it.

Oh, no! Here comes that blasphemy lecture I had been expecting for years.

But that wasn't the problem at all. The problem, she said: "He's not big enough."

Well then, let's make him grow some more.

The most effective way for me to envision God is to make him flexible, adaptable to my whim of the day. Yes, I'm a Gemini. We're big on whims.

One day God is nature. The next day he's a blue stick-figure man but giant.

Another day he's infused in EVERYTHING. Those days are probably the best. They also lead to some interesting conversations.

"What do you mean, God is in the doorknob?"

No matter what details change, several things remain constant. Like the fact that God cares about me. I only needed to look back on the many times I should have been dead to prove that one.

That God is love, light and everything that makes my heart feel good. And that God's will doesn't have to be some mysterious, complex phenomenon. All he really wants? For me to be happy, joyous and free.

God wants EVERYONE to be happy, joyous and free. But we're so busy being human, trying to run our own lives, and believing all the spoon-fed pablum that gets shoved down our throats, that we end up being sad, miserable, and trapped by our mind-forged manacles.

Whoa is right.

*.....LESSONS LEARNEd......e

God rocks. Especially when this Great Spirit can be whatever you want it to be.

Sept. 11

Just like leaving Morty had been only a matter of time, so was leaving New York City. When I first ran away to New York, the fast-paced, chaotic energy fed me. But now it was feeding ON me.

Not only that, but the whole vibe of the city had changed since September 11. Yeah, I had been living in Brooklyn on September 11, 2001. The first plane hit while I was on my way to work at a politician's office (don't ask).

Anyway, I used to ride my bicycle to work, taking the long way so I could pedal along the waterfront and make a pit stop at Brooklyn's 69th Street pier.

Officially known as American Veterans Memorial Pier, the place was a popular fishing spot. I liked hanging out for a spell to absorb the soothing energy and glory of the surrounding water.

On a clear day you could see New Jersey – not kidding! You also had a view of the mighty Verrazano Narrows Bridge, the Statue of Liberty, and One World Trade Center.

On that fateful morning, a billowing plume of smoke caught my eye in the direction of the Trade Center.

Wow, I thought. There's a lot of pollution today. The smoke was actually coming OUT of a Trade Center building – but something in my mind still chalked it up to pollution.

Maybe someone installed a mini factory in the basement? Maybe it was somehow being blown there from a facility in New Jersey?

When the brain can't comprehend something, it starts scrambling for any type of explanation.

I got back on my bike and pedaled the rest of the way to the Bensonhurst office – only to walk in to a total madhouse. The radio was on. Staff members were running around like headless chickens. Politician man kept saying something about "National emergency, national emergency!"

"What the heck is going on?" I asked.

"The World Trade Center has just been bombed!"

I remembered a bomb exploding in the parking garage beneath the World Trade Center in 1993. The thing ripped a massive crater into the floors above and ground below. Six people were killed. Sigh. Not another terrorist attack like this, I thought. But Sept. 11 was nothing like that.

"The whole tower just went down!" a coworker screamed.

That's when my brain went "click" and slammed shut. It was its attempt at protecting my sanity. It simply refused to believe it.

There is NO WAY that could happen. NO WAY. No way. NO WAY. It was simply too absurd to fathom.

We were all sent home for the day. I immediately wrote a poem – or it wrote itself. I started my very first website. I had to do something, anything so I wouldn't just sit there with my mouth gaping open in shock and disbelief.

CHASTISED
In the wake of the World Trade Center disaster

I wasn't born yet
for the Kennedy thing but this morning
on the 69th Street Pier I saw the
smoke billow out from the World Trade Center
across the way but chalked it up to
being no big deal since I had just
written a poem about pollution.

I found out
I was wrong.

It hit me first
at work
when I heard the news that a plane came
hijacked from Boston to New York and I thought
of my brother, although he lived in Boston several lives
ago, I wanted to know he was ok but

nothing was ok. Nothing was alright and then
the lady's voice on 1010 declared the second
tower came town and that didn't hit me yet
until I heard Manhattan now has
a new skyline...

I thought of my
drawings I must redo as I
answered the e-mails from frantic friends
still in Michigan typing in all caps
PLEASE TELL ME YOU'RE OK and it
hit me again

on the ride home on my bike
since my boss – and the Senate – declared it time to close
after
hearing – six times – this is a national emergency and he

offered to drive all of us home, me and my bike if I
took off the tire and I was
about to accept when he
locked the keys in his car so I pedaled – cautiously –
through the dampered streets, past another guy
on a bike wearing a bright white surgical mask and
thought, since I smoke, if I did the same thing I would feel
like a hypocrite I feel

we have a glimpse
of WWIII never mind Archduke
Ferdinand the Third or the shot heard round the world I just
heard
the radio bleed that the Arabs on the West Bank
are handing out candy, they are having a party, saying that
God is good there is death in America,
the garden-shaped wuss we could all blame Bush
and hummus and indigo things but I don't know enough to jab

or point political fingers – I only know enough
to know that
I am scared

and I only know enough to hope that the
slumbering oaf we call a country
stirs itself awake enough
to rear its massive head
in prayer.

-Ryn Gargulinski, Sept. 11, 2001

I remained in denial for weeks. Months. Maybe even a year or two.

Refused to look out the window of the overhead subway train like I used to when we were heading over the bridge from Brooklyn to Manhattan. That way I wouldn't have to see the big hole where two Trade Center towers once stood.

Although I knew it happened on a logical level, my brain was still extremely confused that something like this actually occurred.

Even when I'd see debris from the explosion wash up on the shore of Coney Island beach. Even when an ashen pall hung in the atmosphere for weeks. Even when, years later, my parents and I paid a visit to a memorial in-the-making at Ground Zero.

I didn't know anyone who had been killed in the tragedy. But it still hurt like hell. Was scary as hell. It ripped out the entire foundation of my sense of security. Safety. Trust. Freedom.

I felt violated and vulnerable – like it could happen again at anytime, anywhere throughout the city. I put a pause on my habit of walking over the Brooklyn Bridge.

Bomb scares became a regular thing, especially around my job in midtown Manhattan. It seemed subways were consistently evacuated. Streets cordoned off with the royal blue New York City Police Department wooden barricades.

You could taste the fear the minute you left the house. And more often than not, it even followed you home.

*.....LESSONS LEARNED......e

Security in the outer world is a total myth. That's why we need to find it within.

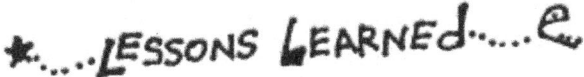

Escape from NY

I had been toying with the idea of leaving New York for some time, but it really hit home when I was coming home from splurging on a yoga retreat in Tulum, Mexico. The New York skyline came into view as the plane was coming in for a landing. The moment I saw all cold metal and concrete, I started to cry.

No, I couldn't live here anymore. I couldn't do what I was doing anymore. Not unlike drinking, all this non-creative administrative stuff at my Madison Avenue job was killing my soul.

I was definitely not doing what I loved. I loved to write. I loved to draw. I loved to be creative. I didn't love filling out and filing paperwork.

My boss was a gem. He saw I needed more to keep me going, came up with little pockets of creative things for me to do. Even paid for me to study to get my own state license to sell life insurance.

I sold one policy right off the bat. Actually, the policy sold itself. A friend was in the midst of a divorce and needed to ensure her kids were secure. I was waiting for some kind of rush of something to give me a sign that selling life insurance was indeed a groove a could get into.

Just like that parade I was sure was going to march down the street to celebrate my first year sober, it never came.

I was doing freelance writing on the side, had a few columns published in a couple of NYC papers, a weekly column in a Brooklyn publication. Covered some news stories for a group of local papers.

This was back when newspapers were cool and actually reported news. Before the internet got ahold and turned journalism into a joke.

My experience had been fun, but it wasn't enough to land me a gig at the "New York Daily News" or, even better, the "New York Post." It might be enough, however, to get a job at small-town paper where I could gain more experience and then work my way upward.

I started responding to help wanted posts at JournalismJobs.com.

The Bahamas, yes. Florida, yes. Idaho, no. Montana, no. Hawaii, hell yes. Michigan, no – been there, done that. Ohio, no; probably just like Michigan.

Nevada? Nah. Don't like gambling. New Mexico, yeah, that one sounds good. I could sell all my faux fur coats and boots since it's hot and sunny all year round, right?

My applications must have been written in invisible ink that disappeared when it hit the recipients' inboxes. All those emails to places all over the world, and nary a reply.

That's it. I'm destined to sell life insurance from the seventh floor of a Madison Avenue building for the rest of my life. A dress code memo on my desk every Monday. Little boxes on life insurance forms that don't even have enough room to fill in the info. A pile of things to be filed all week long.

I cried. I despaired. I wondered how I could get around the dress code thing and once again wear flip-flops to the office. Then I got a response from one really cool editor who was willing to give me a chance.

Clovis, New Mexico, here I come!

★·····LESSONS LEARNED······℮

We change. Things change. Places change. We're happiest if we accept or even fall in love with what is, not pine for what once was.

Should I Stay or Should I Go?

The decision. The big, fat decision. It was time to make it.

The whooshing excitement of moving to New Mexico to be a full-time journalist sent little happy tremors all the way to the tips of my toes. Until it was abruptly blocked by my old nemesis.

You guessed it. Fear.

Yes. No? No. Yes?

New Mexico and a brand-new start, doing what I loved, would be an absolute thrill. But I would be leaving behind everything and everyone I had known for the past 17 years.

I was again pulled into the false sense of security that comes from staying with the misery I knew – versus making a massively monumental change that would alter the course of my life forever.

Of course, there are those things called baby steps that could have slowly and gently acclimated me to changes.

But what fun is that? Why merely wiggle a loose tooth when you can wrench it out with pliers in one fell swoop?

Life is never boring when you happen to be an extremist.

The cool New Mexico editor had given me ample time to make my decision. I even flew to New Mexico to check it out before fully committing to moving there (a total Mom idea. I typically don't have time to do all kinds of sensible things like that).

Making decisions was one of the toughest things I was facing in recovery. Now I had to think for myself. It was dang hard.

When I was drinking, I just shuttled all the decisions on to Morty. So much so, I even gave him my bank cards and told him to make all the financial decisions. When he finally gave them back upon on our split, I was aghast.

"What???!!!!! There's a total of $8 in my savings account? I trusted you blah blah I've been so wronged blah blah how am I supposed to live on $8 blah blah what did you do with all the money?!!!"

"Ryn," he said coolly and calmly. "How else could I have kept you swimming in beer?"

Oh.

For months after leaving Morty, I still fought the urge to call him every time I had to make a choice.

Should I take the local subway train or wait for the express? Will that potato print of hot pink rat silhouettes I made that one drunken night look stupid hanging in my new living room? What should I have for lunch?

What color socks should I wear? (For the record, all my socks were either grey or black.)

Every time I fought the urge to call Morty for an answer, I had to find someone else to make my decisions. I even tried it with a coworker, asked him to come shopping with me for a TV for my new apartment.

"Which one should I get – this one or that one?"

"I'm not making that decision for you," he said. "Then you'll just blame me when you end up wishing you bought the other one."

Dagnabbit. It always irked me when people were on to my games.

Apparently this coworker was out of the running for the New Mexico question. So I asked everyone else I knew instead.

People that liked me told me to stay. People that didn't told me to move. And then there were others who had no clue. About anything.

"New Mexico?" one woman had responded. "Do you have a passport? Do you speak the language?"

I deleted her number off my contact list.

✶·····LESSONS LEARNED·······℮

There are no "right" or "wrong" decisions. Only some that may be wiser than others. And some that are so much more fun.

Get out of your head and into your heart when you need guidance on what to decide.

Part 3
Beyond My Wildest Dreams

There's something wrong
with what you're doing
if you're not having fun.

-Ryn Gargulinski, 2005

New Mexico – 2005

Wow. It was April and already something like 70 degrees in Clovis, New Mexico. It didn't get the Land of Enchantment nickname for nothing. Actually, it got the Land of Enchantment nickname as a backup.

Whoever was supposed to make the original state motto official never did, so Florida stole it. The Sunshine State. You can still find old souvenir ashtrays that call New Mexico the Sunshine State. Or at least I did. That's not the only thing I found in this enchanting place.

Yes, I decided to move. I'm glad I had stockpiled savings leading up to the choice. The movers alone cost more than $5,000. For a one-bedroom Brooklyn apartment with a single closet – that somehow managed to take up some 250 moving boxes.

Then there was the plane fare, the deposit on the rental house, household items to use while I waited the six weeks for the movers to finally bring my things.

Don't forget a car. I didn't drive at all in New York City, which is probably the only reason my record wasn't littered with drunk driving charges.

I had to buy a car, a major investment. Especially since Mom agreed to sell me her old car, a Pontiac Grand Prix, for $1. Oh, and the cost of hauling it from Michigan to New Mexico on a big ole car carrier.

So, I was set and on my way to a brand-new life. I am so glad all the basics were in place, because the culture shock started blowing my mind immediately, lasting for at least six months.

I went from big, tall, noisy concrete jungle with zooms and bangs and sirens and screams and everyone moving at 573 mph – to a place I had to wait 20 minutes just to get a cup of coffee at the Circle K.

And that wasn't because it was crowded, but because the cashier and single customer ahead of me were chatting about this that and the other thing until the cows came home.

Circle K was the Clovis equivalent to New York City bodegas. Except they also sold gas. And the main location stopped making coffee at 10 a.m.

I was used to subways, buses, bicycling or walking everywhere, typically racking up 30,000+ steps per day on my pedometer. Walking around in Clovis was rare enough for someone to pull over to ask if you needed a ride, as your car must have petered out somewhere along Gunstock Road.

While I thought I'd get the same kind of outcast treatment for my weirdness that I got in suburban Michigan, I didn't. People were so friendly, it made me cry at least twice.

A farmer man and his wife let me – a total stranger with sticking-up hair – spend the night at their house when I couldn't find a motel room while covering my first story in Milnesand, New Mexico.

It was the annual Prairie Chicken Festival and, little did I know, you needed to secure a motel room months in advance to beat the crowds.

Some people showed up with tents so they could just sleep in a field while they were waiting for the big event. That event was riding in a gutted van out into the middle of the boondocks at three in the morning to watch the prairie chickens do their ritual mating dance at dawn.

I am not kidding. That was a big thing in New Mexico.

I absolutely loved it.

It was so refreshing not to put up with shoving on the subway trains and filing paperwork in a stuffy Madison Avenue office. Now I spent my days writing about prairie chickens, attending council meetings where members showed up in cowboy hats and boots, and said a prayer before the meeting started.

I eventually got a weekly column (yaay!), where I wrote about the culture shock that made you feel like you were inside some kind of Southwestern surrealist painting.

I tried to slow down my hurried pace, a tough call after nearly two decades of scurrying and pushing through the streets as if my hair, pants and shoes were on fire.

I grew a garden with giant sunflowers in my Clovis yard. I marveled at the stars, the millions of billions of stars in the sky that New York bright lights and skyscrapers muted from view.

I even learned how to use a lawn mower, which was a good thing and a bad thing. A good thing because, well, I could mow my lawn. A bad thing because that's how I met the guy I dubbed Mr. New Mexico.

Another big change from New York to New Mexico was the recovery meetings. While I was used to having an array of hundreds of meetings at all times of the day and night from which to choose, I only found a small handful in Clovis.

I set up a schedule to attend the one or two I liked most. Got to know the people and liked them immediately, especially since they thought I was all intriguing and glamorous since I had just come from New York City. OK, maybe not all that intriguing and glamorous. But one woman did say she liked my shoes.

"Where did you get those shoes?! I need some!"

"Um, somewhere on Broadway near Canal Street. But maybe they deliver?"

These were the days before online shopping was the way of the world, the good ole days before my monthly Amazon bill consistently cost more than my rent payment.

One dude at the meeting was one of those I'm-too-cool-for-this types. He'd come in the meetings late, proceed to prop his dusty hiking boots up on the table, then lean back on his chair with his sunglasses on, chewing gum.

What an ass, I thought. I'm staying away from that guy. It got even worse when he'd brag about his exploits.

"I use women and take all their money," he said.

We moved in together three weeks later.

★......LESSONS LEARNED......

You'll keep getting the same lessons again and again until you finally learn them. Apparently my relationship learning curve was steep.

Goats

I'm not sure if it was my need for love, my need to be codependent, or the need for someone to show me how to use a lawn mower, but I got into a number of relationships that were, shall we say, less than ideal.

I was somehow drawn to people who ended up being no good for me and treating me like garbage. Looking back, I totally understand that my own self-worth was still at the bottom of the gutter.

Since I still thought of myself as garbage, it makes sense I would pick people who treated me like garbage.

But I didn't get that at the time these relationships were going on. I would instead endure whatever disrespect came my way, rationalizing their behavior.

Maybe Mr. New Mexico had a neck issue that made him ogle women over my shoulder while I was trying to talk to him at the bus stop.

Perhaps he had some kind of chemical imbalance that made him sneak outside to smoke and flirt with the waitress when I went to the bathroom during our dinner out.

Or maybe he was, as I initially predicted, just an ass.

I got a New Mexico sponsor. She hated him immediately.

"I know what guys like that are all about," said the happily married tow truck driver. Yeah, she was cool.

Mr. New Mexico didn't like her, either. Probably because she knew what guys like that were all about.

Regardless, Mr. New Mexico and I stayed together. He even made the big move to Tucumcari with me when I was promoted to managing editor of the Quay County paper.

This position was a whirlwind of learning. I wrote the news, features and my column. I took photos, attended meetings with the cowboy boots people, and even learned how to do newspaper layout.

With its tile floors and echo-ey walls, the newspaper office kind of reminded me of an old person's basement. And supposedly there was an old man haunting the office, just to make things more exciting.

I was digging the job and, despite the fact that I had to drive Mr. New Mexico everywhere because he had lost his license, having fun on the home front. I got a puppy named Lulu. A rental house that was an old farmhouse with a massive yard, giant trees, and a readymade enclosed pen.

I needed something to keep in the pen. I went with goats.

You'd think it would be easy to get goats in rural New Mexico, right? But it really wasn't. We asked around to the ends of the county and back, but the best we could find was an old mean nanny goat.

I'll take her.

Not only was she mean and old, but she was also a one-trick pony, so to speak. She was insistent on doing one thing and one thing only, and she did it all day long. That thing was hopping the fence.

It got to be a joke at work. The minute the front office woman would hear the sheriff on the phone, she'd immediately transfer the call back to me.

"Ma'am," the sheriff would tell me, "Your goat is out wandering the streets again."

This was cutting into my work time. Mean old nanny had to go.

The woman who gave us mean old nanny took her back, giving me two of her children instead. The goat's children, not the woman's children. A boy and a girl. Mr. New Mexico tricked me into naming them Slim and Shady. I had no idea that was Eminem's nickname.

I fell in love with the two kids immediately. They seemed to enjoy me, too.

They'd give me back massages by pounding their hooves on my back. They shared sips of my morning coffee. They went absolutely gaga for Kentucky Fried Chicken biscuits, as if it were manna from the sky.

The column I wrote about their fascination with their biscuits ended up framed on the wall at the local KFC. Pretty cool indeed.

I fell in love with these goats enough to invite them into our house one night. Well, I didn't really have a choice. It was either that or let them drown.

The sky had opened up to release flood-level rain that was lasting for hours. I watched the goat pen start flooding. The water level quickly reached the goats' knees. Then it was up to their chests.

When I looked up the next time, I only saw Slim. He was suddenly atop something in the water, something tall enough for him to be above water while most everything else was below it.

That thing was Shady's back. Only her little head was visible above the water line, with her neck pointed upwards to keep breathing for as long as possible as the water was rapidly reaching her chin.

I quickly turned the laundry room into a makeshift goat pen. Everything that could possibly be chewed was removed. Or so I thought. That left a washer, a dryer and enough room for the goats to stand up, lie down and even move around a bit.

The room didn't have a door, so I pulled a giant recliner to block the doorway to the kitchen. Then Mr. New Mexico went out and retrieved the goats from the rain. It was like a scene from a Noah's Ark movie.

The rain was slashing the sky as Mr. New Mexico ran headlong into the sloshing water, coming back with one goat, then the other. Now he just had to get two of every other species on earth.

Putting two rambunctious goats in your laundry room is not a good idea. It was a whole night of banging, clanging and putting a table in front of the recliner so they'd stop kicking it out of the doorway.

By morning the room was trashed. The washer had a dent in it. They had somehow managed to pull the aluminum dryer vent hose out from behind the dryer. It was now chewed to shreds. Guess they wanted it to match the back of the recliner, which they shredded with their hooves.

It took about five hours of scrubbing and 15 buckets of cleanser to get the goat pee smell out of the room. Then I got an added bonus. When I went outside to dump the last bucket of cleanup water, I noticed my car window had been partially open throughout the entire night-long downpour.

Then one day – alas! – the goats were missing!

No, no! Please don't let them be wandering things like their mother.

Called the sheriff to see if he had any goat sightings. Nope.

They weren't in the pen. They weren't in the yard. They weren't in the laundry room (thank God). They weren't wandering the streets.

Where the hell were they?

That's when I heard a big-loud "Baaaaaaaa" coming from up in the sky. I looked up. They had both climbed and were hanging out in the giant tree.

Hilarious, but also curious. Why didn't they climb up the tree to avoid drowning in the flood? I bet it was a ploy just to get into the house to eat the dryer hose.

Less hilarious was the Halloween night when two demons invaded the goat pen. Demons have always been real to me. I have no doubt they're romping around this earth, trying to pull us into their depths of darkness.

They already got me once, with my addiction to alcohol. The downward spiral eroded my body, brain, heart and soul, left me bleeding on death's door at the age of 29.

Any addiction that drags you to the pits of hell can go into devil category, like those zombies that roamed vacant lots and crouched in abandoned buildings in my early days in New York City.

Chicken Man Dan had a big dose of evil in him. Seems a prerequisite when you chop up and boil your roommate. Johann may have been in cahoots with the devil, as were those shadow people who told me to poke out my eye with a wire hanger as a kid.

I never knew what shadow people were until I saw medium Amy Allan talk about them on her "Dead Files" show. These wicked entities like to prey on children, trying to talk them into doing self-destructive things. They tried to coerce her to chew on a plugged-in electrical cord.

So yes, I knew demonic beings were out there. Being sober and living in the light had kept much of the demonic stuff at bay. But there I was, on Halloween night no less, with creepy creatures lurking in the darkness.

Mr. New Mexico noticed them first.

"There's something with yellow glowing eyes out there," he told me.

"Ha, ha," I responded. "Good try. Good trick for Halloween."

"No, really," he insisted. I looked. He was right. Glowing yellow eyes with black slit pupils, really low off the ground. Short monsters? Tall serpents? A couple of adolescent Chupacabra lying on their sides?

"Demons, demons, demons!" I think we screamed it in unison and ran in the house. Now we had a huge decision to make.

Do we get the flashlight for a closer look, or do we barricade ourselves in the bedroom and light a bunch of sage?

Since we didn't have sage, we went for the flashlight.

Slowly, carefully, we crept back out into the darkness. The yellow eyes stared, unblinking, in our direction. We moved closer, closer, shone the flashlight in their direction.

Two of the cutest little pygmy goats stared back at us. "Baaaaa."

Apparently, one of the guys Mr. New Mexico had hit up for goats finally delivered two of them, some five months later. They were even more adorable in the morning sunlight. I forget what we named them, but I know it wasn't after a rap star.

And I remember we named their child Ryn. Yes, the female pygmy gave birth a week or so after they showed up.

I heard horrific bleating noises coming from the pen one afternoon. Ran outside to check it out. Slim, Shady and Mr. Pygmy were all standing around Mrs. Pygmy – who was in the midst of having a baby.

I wasn't sure what the heck was going on at first, since all I saw was chaos and a lot of blood. I thought I had a murder on my hands. But it was quite the opposite. It was a new life.

The moment the baby goat was on the ground, all the other goats started screaming and kicking at it.

What?! Maybe they ARE demons after all.

I ran back inside, grabbed something to cut the umbilical cord and a towel to wipe up the blood mess. I snipped the cord. The blood mess wouldn't budge. So I brought the baby inside, rinsing her little white goat body in the bathtub.

Awww, there was absolutely nothing demonic about this darling little creature!

I remember Grandpa P once scolding me for touching a butterfly. He said it made them crippled and if I touched it, I would kill it.

Way to go, me.

I carried that guilt for years. I was praying and hoping that same theory didn't apply to baby goats.

When I took baby goat Ryn back out to the pen, Mrs. Pygmy was fine with the reunion. But the other goats were not. They immediately started screaming and kicking at the baby.

My dear Baby Ryn goat!

Enough was enough of that. Mrs. Pygmy and Baby Ryn got their own private pen we constructed with wood stakes and chicken wire, beneath the shade of a big happy tree.

All was pretty blissful after that, or at least as blissful as things can be with a guy who drooled every time he saw another woman. All was blissful, that is, until two more incidents came along to upset the proverbial applecart.

Well, make that three if you count the castration. I agreed with Mr. New Mexico that five goats were more than enough. I also agreed it would be good idea to have Sir Pygmy goat get fixed so we'd have no more babies to worry about.

I just didn't realize Mr. New Mexico would do it himself, with a rubber band and a Leatherman all-purpose tool. Yikes. If you thought the bleating was loud and horrific when the goats were attacking a baby, you should have heard the screams Sir Pygmy made when he was being fixed from having one.

If I would have known that was the method, I would have definitely tracked down a goat vet instead.

Sigh. The second hellish incident brought back all those fond memories and emotions of being the stared-at, pointed-at outcast. That's what I had suddenly become for some reason, and I didn't even know why.

I had gone to a morning routine doctor's appointment, and the entire waiting room fell silent the moment I walked in. All sets of eyes were on me, steely and cold, slicing through my soul.

Thankfully I was called in for my appointment quickly, was able to go through the blah blah blah, and then zoom on outta there to the newspaper office.

Editor boss in Clovis called soon after I arrived.

Don't recall his exact words, but it was something like: "I heard you went from newspaper darling to most hated in Tucumcari."

"I noticed that at the doctor's office," I said in a panic. "What happened?"

"Your last column."

Ohhhhhh. Wow. It was Christmastime and I had been scratching my brain for a topic that wasn't the same-old played-out Merry Christmas stuff. I found it in a "New York Post" story about this this guy who had decorated his yard with Santa depicted as a serial killer.

The man put fake blood all over the snow, put Santa in the middle of it all with a meat cleaver, and hung decapitated Barbie dolls from the nearby trees and eaves.

I thought it might be fun to write about that. Figured it would be a refreshing change from the usual happy-pappy holiday stuff.

Evidently, the paper's readership didn't agree. It took a loooong time to live that one down. But at least I didn't get beat up or fired. Whew. And I still won Best Humor Column in New Mexico for two years in a row – for submissions that didn't include the bloody Santa.

The third incident that burst the bliss bubble in Tucumcari was also the one that had me packing my bags and moving even further west. A teen boy showed up on our doorstep with a duffel bag. It was Mr. New Mexico's son.

What?

I knew he had two children. But I also knew they were far away, living with their mother, a distant ex. Apparently the teen boy became too much for her. So she found out where Mr. New Mexico lived, gave the kid a plane ticket, and gave him the old cliché: "Go live with your father."

What?

No, no, no! I'm way too young to be a stepmother.

Visions of my youth instantly flitted away. I thought the minute you were branded a stepmother you suddenly became old, wrinkled, evil and prone to making your stepchildren sweep out the chimney.

We had no chimney. But it wasn't long before I had the 16-year-old in tears, raking up the goat poo in the goat pen.

I had made a list of house rules to set the stage. They weren't impossible, even for a teen. We already knew he smoked. So I told him we all smoked outside the house. If you want a cigarette, go outside. He instead decided to smoke in the room we gave him, hiding the ashtray under the bed.

Goat pen duty for you!

It wasn't being mean. It was common sense. The house was old and rickety and not mine. It wouldn't really be a good idea to burn it down. It's enough the laundry room was still recovering from 52 gallons of goat urine.

Common sense or not, I later realized I was a selfish mess who didn't want the kid around. Thus, I'd do anything I could to make him go away. The problem was, his mom wasn't taking him back. Living with Mr. New Mexico's parents, the boy's grandparents, would work – but Mr. New Mexico would have to go with him.

Mr. New Mexico and I got into a big blowup over the son, and I finally gave him another old cliché: "It's him or me."

He picked the son.

Goodbye, New Mexico. Hello, sunny California.

Except where I was moving wasn't sunny at all. To show Mr. New Mexico the error of his ways, I had to move somewhere far, and fast.

I'll show him!

I scrambled around answering journalism job postings that were at least 600 miles from Tucumcari. I had even considered Alaska.

One editor called me right away, interviewed me on the phone, and then hired me on the spot. It was a reporter job in Northern California.

After I accepted with glee, we chatted a bit before bringing the call to a close. He said five little words as we were hanging up, words that made my stomach drop to the soles of my feet.

"I hope you like rain."

I don't. I hate it. It makes me sad and makes goats eat dryer hose.

Now what had I gotten myself into?

✱.....LESSONS LEARNED......℮

When recovery promises a life beyond your wildest dreams, you may automatically think riches and fame. But it could just as easily be New Mexico and goats. I wouldn't have dreamed up either one in a million zillion years.

Pacific Northwest – 2006

Beautiful Gasquet, California, was as Northern California as you could get. In the middle of the Redwood Forest. Less than 10 miles south of the Oregon border. About 15 miles inland from my newspaper job in Crescent City.

Gasquet had pine trees. Redwood trees. Moss, ferns, those lichen things that look like elfin staircases winding around the stumps. Mountains. A random air strip where private planes would land from time to time.

The whole town's population was 400, according to the welcome sign. When my parents came to visit, Dad asked if they changed it to 401 when I moved in. Mom and Dad came to visit after I had already gotten a dog and was at the beginning of my next fateful relationship.

While most of the Gasquet homes were log cabins with bears or eagles carved out of giant redwood trunks in their sprawling front yard, it also had a small apartment complex with about six units. That was my new home. The weight limit on pets was 30 pounds, so dog Lulu stayed behind with Mr. New Mexico.

My new dog was a purebred Miniature Pincher named Zola, a good 15 pounds below the 30-pound limit. She was adorable, high-strung and barked at absolutely everything. Even better, when she heard a siren while we were driving in the car, she'd wail like a banshee being skinned.

Blaine despised her. Blaine was my bad relationship du jour, as it seemed I couldn't move anywhere without picking some guy who would act like a jerk, treat me like crap, and then give me the perfect excuse to flee the state.

I promised myself I wouldn't date any recovery people for a while, since neither Johann nor Mr. New Mexico had worked out all that well. I should have instead promised myself I wouldn't date any people for a while. But I met Blaine by chance while Zola and I were hanging out by the river.

She started barking at him immediately. He pretended it was delightfully funny. We chatted. He laughed at my jokes. He was big and strong and muscular. He was also a long-time area resident – if you count his 10 years in the nearby Pelican Bay State Prison as a residency.

Yeah, I was dating an ex-con. But this time I played it safe. I didn't invite him to move in with me within the first month. I waited for at least month two.

My parents came to visit while I was in the early stages of the relationship with Blaine. I had invited him to come hang out with us. Despite making amends to my parents, I still felt uncomfortable around them. I thought Blaine would make a good buffer.

Mom called me on it, out of Blaine's earshot, nearly immediately.

"Are we that bad to visit with that you have to ask this stranger to come along?"

"That's not it," I insisted, even though it was. Actually, they weren't bad to visit with. I was just uncomfortable doing it.

My parents were too smart sometimes. Especially when it came to their first impression of Blaine. They hated him immediately.

Since it was sunny and hot in Gasquet, but cold and windy at the coast, I wanted to hang out by the river in the sun. Mom and Dad wanted to go see what was happening for the Fourth of July weekend in Crescent City.

I ended up with Zola and Blaine by the river. My parents ended up at cow puck bingo.

Just when you thought a New Mexico prairie chicken festival was high entertainment, the Pacific Northwest one-ups it with cow puck bingo.

Yes, it's just like it says. You get a bingo board and can mark off a square if one of the cows wandering around a grid in the field poops in the square that's on your board.

Bingo!

I remember two things most about my parents' visit. One was Dad coming close to swearing in the middle of the night. Dad was the strong and silent type, so him almost swearing was a big deal.

He never complained about anything, either. Except the one time in New York when I thought it would be a great idea for me, Mom and Dad to walk the 70 or so blocks to Coney Island from my Brooklyn apartment. In the searing summer heat. Directly beneath the overhead tracks of an air-conditioned subway train, no less.

Every time a train went by overhead, Mom and Dad would say "We could be on that train, you know."

"No, let's keep walking," said I. "This is great."

The sun blazed. The sweat poured. The sidewalks seemed to get longer and more blinding white with every block. When we finally made it to Nathans at Coney Island, we placed our hot dog orders and then went outside to find a seat at one of the umbrella-shaded plastic picnic tables.

There were no seats. It was standing room only. People were standing around eating hot dogs, leaning on bar-height counters. Dad stood there, a hot dog in each hand, sweat streaming down his brow. He looked around and said two words that I'll remember forever.

"This sucks!"

He never said "sucks." Well, until then. He never swore or even nearly swore, either. Until one night in Gasquet. He uttered a cough in his sleep, sending Zola into a nonstop barking frenzy.

"Jesus Christ," said Dad.

I was so honored to have been present in situations that made a man who never complained or swear begin to complain and near-swear.

The second thing I remember most about my parents' visit was feeling like a real jerk. Probably because I acted like one. I still feel awful my parents came all the way from Michigan to visit and I chose to spend a day with Blaine instead of them.

My parents and I did spend time together during their visit, but I still feel like a heel for going to the river that day. Especially since I missed cow puck bingo. And double especially because Blaine turned out to be one of the biggest mistakes of my life.

★.....LESSONS LEARNED......☙

Did I mention you'll keep getting the same lessons again and again until you finally learn them…and that my relationship learning curve was steep?

The Ex-Con and a Cat

Having a stalker in my past at least made it easier to spot the signs of a relationship that could turn deadly. Blaine was one of them. I was done with the Blaine thing nearly as quickly as it started. But there was one problem.

By now he was living in my apartment.

Blaine moving in with me was a bad idea, which I felt yet still ignored the minute he started hinting he needed a place to live.

"My roommate and I aren't getting along," he told me. "It would just be until I found somewhere else to live."

The damn people-pleasing habit once again got the best of me.

"OK, sure," I said. "Let's give it a go."

The situation was a mess right from the start. It ended up his roommate was his long-time girlfriend and mother of his 6-month-old child. All three had been living in a trailer park. I found this out when he asked me to help him retrieve some of his stuff and I saw framed photos of the trio all over the trailer.

That was red flag number two. (Red flag number one had been the ex-con status.)

He gathered up all kinds of stuff, including a VCR with the woman's name written on it with hot pink nail polish.

"She owes me," he said. Red flag number three.

He insisted he bring his cat, which was not trained to use a litter box.

"We just leave the window open and the screen off so the cat can go in and out as she needs to," he explained. Red flag number four.

My Gasquet apartment was on the first floor in the middle of the forest. I read enough true crime to know the forest can be the perfect hunting ground for serial killers.

Not only that, but I think I saw Big Foot one night while driving home on the pitch-black winding road through the trees. Something loping, hunched and gargantuan had appeared and then disappeared out of the corner of my eye.

Yeah, let's leave the window open and the screen off.

Despite the red flags popping up like Whac-A-Mole, he moved in anyway. Sigh. My pattern of people pleasing wasn't fully apparent to me at the time, but I can easily see it in hindsight.

Isn't that always the way? I put a higher priority on making others happy than on making myself happy, or even doing things that were good for me. I wanted people to like me. I wanted people to love me. I wanted to feel like I belonged, things I didn't have in the past, especially in that hell called high school.

If you really want to play the blame game (which the victim-mentality people are REALLY good at), we could blame the nasty cliques that excluded me in high school for my ready agreement at letting an ex-con infiltrate my life. But we're not. So we won't.

I'll instead take full responsibility for allowing my people-pleasing habit to cloud my judgement, for letting Blaine and his untrained cat move in.

Zola hated it, barking even more than usual. I hated it, crying when no one was looking. And evidently Blaine's cat hated it, too.

The first thing the cat did was claw a hole in my giant inflatable exercise ball that I used as a desk chair. The second thing it did was somehow smear a big wad of cat poo in the middle of the wall.

I didn't see either thing happen, but I did walk into the room I used as an office-gym to find a deflated heap of exercise ball and a streak of poop about 12 inches long. Maybe Blaine had tried to clean it up so I wouldn't notice?

I noticed. I grumbled as I washed it off the wall. I also brought both issues to his attention when he came home from his midnight shift.

"What are you talking about?" he asked with one of those incredulous faces with bulging eyes and a wide-open mouth. I was hoping a fly would fly in his mouth. Lord knows they had the opportunity, with the screen off the open window.

"My cat would NEVER do that," he insisted. "Where's the cat poop? I don't even see it?!"

"That's because I already cleaned it up," I explained. "You think I'm going to leave a streak of cat poo on the wall?"

"You're crazy. You're just crazy. There WAS no cat poop on the wall. And your exercise ball was deflated before I even moved in."

"No, it wasn't," I insisted.

"Yes, it was. You're just crazy."

Would you believe my self-esteem was so low and my intuition so ignored that I started toying with the idea that he may be right? That the ball HAD been deflated and the cat poop swoosh had just been a figment of my imagination?

Stop this now.

I had gone crazy twice already, once with the DTs and then again with the depression. I'm not letting some bully make it happen for a third time.

It seemed futile to argue.

"OK, whatever you say, man," I said. Maybe this thing would resolve itself, the same way other things go away if you ignore them. Like your health.

It got to the point where I would do a little happy dance every time he left for work. The cat went back to the "roommate" ex-girlfriend. And Blaine worked long hours on his overnight shift.

Yes, yes, yes!

He was gone most nights. I was at the newspaper office most days. That meant I only had to put up with him for an hour or two in the middle of that while I tried to figure out a way to get him out.

He came up with that way himself one horrible awful night. The night he came home from work after an hour, saw me reading in bed, and decided he wanted to have sex. I didn't. I told him I didn't.

When a 280-pound, meaty slab of a man lies on top of you so heavy you can barely breathe, and then pulls away the covers to get his way, it doesn't matter how many times you say no. He's going to do what he wants.

I did that out-of-the-body thing where you stare at the ceiling and pretend you are somewhere else, anywhere else, anywhere but trapped beneath a heavy, sweaty, grunting thing whose cat somehow smears its excrement on your wall.

When he was done, he rolled over and went to sleep. I went into the bathroom to take a shower that felt like it lasted three days.

I also came up with a master plan to get him out. Asking him to leave did not work. Telling him he had to leave didn't work, either. But if the sheriff told him he had to leave, that might be a different story.

I scurried to work as early as possible, got on the phone with the sheriff's office to tell them my predicament.

"No, he's not on the lease. No, we're not married." I went into more gory details. A batch of deputies were sent to make him leave. They said they'd get him out of the apartment for now, and come back to monitor him on whatever day we set up for him to come back and get his things.

Thank you thank you thank you!

A flood of beautiful relief flooded through my veins. But it was quickly replaced with sheer terror.

Zola! My brain kicked into rationalization mode right away.

No. No way. I don't care how gross, sweaty, mean or meat-brained Blaine is, he wouldn't do anything to a teeny dog.

He had a cat, after all. He can't hate animals. Anyone that would hurt an innocent animal is a total monster….is he REALLY that bad?!

I zoomed home as quickly as possible, which wasn't really a zoom at all. It was a slow, meandering drive through the redwoods along the edge of a straight-down cliff. I thought that road was tough in the dark in the rain. But now I was driving it while shaking with panic.

I got to the apartment. Blaine was gone. The deputies were gone.

But Zola, is Zola still here? Oh please, God, tell me yes!

I walked in and saw her tagged collar lying unbuckled in the middle of the floor.

Posters. Long walks through the woods, calling her name. More long walks through the woods. More posters. Knocking on doors throughout Gasquet and beyond.

No one had seen her. I knew they wouldn't. Although I went through the motions of tracking down a lost dog, I knew she wasn't lost. I knew in my heart Blaine had killed her.

I expanded my search to include garbage cans and Dumpsters, other places he may have hurled her little body. I never saw Zola again.

This meaty monster with a wall-pooping cat was messing with the wrong woman. Being stalked back in New York had taught me a thing or two about fighting back against abhorrent bullies (as if bullies came in non-abhorrent varieties).

My first move, after changing the locks, was to get an order of protection against him. While I knew the flimsy piece of paper was not enough to save your life if someone really wanted you dead, it was enough to get the guy arrested if he violated it.

That's why Johann had been thrown in jail at least three times since I had one issued against him. Just call the cops when the guy comes within however many feet of you.

I figured getting an order of protection against Blaine would be just as straightforward. Lord knows I had enough fodder.

It would also be a fun thing for him to explain to his parole officer, maybe enough to send him back into prison. I don't remember if his charge had been attempted murder for bashing some man's skull in or if the guy had actually died. But I do know Blaine had only served 10 years of sentence. Time off for good behavior. Hopefully that was about to change.

The county would surely issue an order of protection without even blinking.

I was wrong. Even being considered for an order of protection involved going to court. Seeing that jackal again. Standing up in front of the entire courtroom and telling my whole sordid story as to why I wanted an order of protection in the first place.

Blaine showed up, all suited up, with a high-priced lawyer at his elbow. I was there with a domestic abuse advocate. My advocate was great support, but neither of us were a match for the slimy lawyer that twisted everything back on me as if it were all my fault.

"You were lying in bed when he came in the room and wanted sex?"

"Yes."

"That means you must have known he was coming home early, and you were in bed waiting for him. You wanted to have sex as much as he did."

"No, I certainly did not."

"Did you tell him 'No?'"

"Yes, I did. Several times."

"You must be mistaken. My client doesn't recall ever hearing you say no."

"I did say no. I said no!"

"You must not have meant it, or this wouldn't have happened. And you were in a relationship with him, yes? It can't be rape if you're in a relationship. Let's go on to the next point, about the dog you 'claim' my client 'harmed' in some way.

"You say the dog was a purebred that cost $600?"

"Yes."

"There you have it. You must have left the dog unattended and someone stole it, knowing how valuable it was."

Case dismissed. Order of protection DENIED.

In the hallway after the hearing, I saw the judge and high-priced lawyer rubbing elbows and laughing, like they were next door neighbors at a barbecue. The good ole boys club. My only solace at that moment was knowing some people will indeed rot in hell.

The party wasn't over yet. The minute I got back to the newspaper office, my desk phone rang. It was a reader who also happened to be in court that morning.

"Oh, my goodness," she said. "My heart was breaking for you. I don't believe you had to go through all that…and you didn't even get the order of protection."

Tears immediately started rolling down my face, which was burning with shame. I know; I know. Despite what the slick and slimy attorney said, it was not my fault I was raped. But it still felt deep in my heart like I did something wrong.

The call was heartfelt and sympathetic. But it also made me realize my time in this small town was over. I couldn't be an effective reporter and columnist going around interviewing people if I thought everyone saw a big "Raped" sign over my head.

I applied to the sister newspaper up north a bit. Sure, it was only some 20 miles away. But it was a whole world away as far as vibes go. The coastal Southern Oregon town of Brookings had a slow-paced, artsy, retirement community vibe. The coastal Northern California town had been regularly referred to as a "trailer park by the sea."

I was hired. I scored new digs. I packed. I got a new dog. A big dog. I would never get a little dog again.

I got a big dog that no one would even think of messing with. A dog that would kill instead of be killed if ever face-to-face with a monster like Blaine.

★....LESSONS LEARNED.....

As horrific as some situations may seem, they can open the door to something wonderful you would not have otherwise found without them.

Sawyer

The dog's name was Sawyer and he was nowhere near my first adoption pick at the dog shelter. I wanted a big, black mean-looking dog. The black fur would match my favorite color clothing. It would also blend in when the dog shed. The mean-looking part would help keep guys like Blaine away.

All the black dogs I saw were either too small or just not right. Too hyper. Too morose. Too jumpy. Too low-key. I felt like Goldilocks at the Humane Society.

Just as I was about to give up, a pal I brought to the kennel piped up.

"What about him?"

He was pointing at the strangest looking beast. A brown, beige and gold brindle dog with a longish snout and a big mane around his head, not unlike a lion.

I suppose I could trim the mane and make him look more like a dog.

The dog had huge paws, long fur and a big, swishy tail. He had the mane around the head and even more fur around the top of his back legs, like he was wearing pantaloons.

"Well, he's kind of weird looking," I said.

"Oh, that's Sawyer," said a Humane Society worker. "We found him as a puppy on the sidewalk. He's been here seven months."

They had no idea what kind of breed he was. Although he had the long hair of a Collie and the overall looks of a Belgian Tervuren, he was about triple the size of either one. And he was still a youngster.

His mane made him look like a lion. His face looked like a long-nosed bear. I knew there were wolves in the area, so I wondered if he was some kind of Collie-Tervuren-lion-bear-dog-wolf crossbreed.

We took him out to interact. My first test was to whisper in his ear to see how he'd react. I sat on the ground next to the dog. Leaned over and told him a big, fat secret:

"Sheeeshel shee shwa shwa shiiishel," or some other such gibberish.

He looked me in the eye, then immediately licked my face.

I had just found my new best friend.

Sawyer ended up being much more than just a best friend. He became my world.

With a sack of bad relationships to my credit, I decided I'd had enough of this dating thing. Well, to be honest, I never actually dated. I just kind of started living with guys a few weeks after meeting them.

Well, enough of that anyway. It would be me and Sawyer against the world. Although he initially didn't seem up to the challenge, since it took him weeks to even get out of his crate.

I had set up the huge dog crate in the bedroom, a crate I had purchased for Zola when she went through her chewing phase. It's never nice to come home to find a sunscreen tube with dog teeth marks and a carpet slathered with SPF 15.

Sawyer took to the crate immediately, bounding for it when I introduced him to his new digs in Oregon. They were pretty cool digs, an ancient cobbled-together farmhouse.

One part of the house used to be an old-time horse and carriage stop. Its adjacent room had been an old-time post office.

Other rooms had been built on over the years. A bedroom with maroon and yellow velvet wallpaper. A big kitchen with a picture window that let you see the ocean on the other side of the road.

A family room with putrid shag carpet and a wood-burning stove. A pink 1960s-era bathroom with a non-working tub. Another bathroom with a makeshift shower. OK, maybe the shower bathroom wasn't all that cool, especially when it started to stink one day.

After two cans of air freshener and three days of exploration, I found a rotting mouse carcass in the bathroom ceiling fan.

All this fun space to romp and play, but Sawyer had made a beeline for the bedroom when I first introduced him to the place. That's after I was able to pry him out from under the dashboard in the car after getting home from the shelter.

He was skittery scared when he entered the house for the first time, but he calmed down immediately when he spied the crate in the bedroom. He lay in the crate. And stayed there for what seemed like months.

I tried to coax him out with love. He stayed in the crate.

I brought him steak, treats and Charlee Bears. He stayed in the crate.

I crawled into the crate to snuggle with him. Then crawled out of the crate to show him that's what you're supposed to do. He watched with mild curiosity. Then stayed in the crate.

I figured kennel life was all he knew for the first seven months of his life. So I cut him some slack. I also figured he'd come out, or he better come out, when it was finally time for him to go outside to the bathroom.

I was right. He slowly, cautiously ventured out of the crate. I tried ushering him out of the bedroom to the front door of the house. He would not have it. He ran back in the crate.

Damn. He ventured out again, slowly, warily, and trotted over to the bedroom window. The window was actually more like a door wall, tall and wide and nearly reaching the floor. There were no screens on the windows of this old-time farm house. The second I opened the window, he jumped out to the fenced backyard.

Yaay! He romped and played. He rolled around in the dewy green Oregon grass. He chewed on a stick. He chewed on another stick. It started getting dark. It was time to go back inside.

He looked at me like I was insane. The look wasn't necessarily because he wanted to stay outside and chew on a third stick (although that certainly could have been part of it). It was because I was trying to lead him out of the backyard toward the front door.

He was having none of it. No way would he walk through the house. He wanted to go back in through the bedroom window.

While jumping out of the window was easy-peasy because the window was near the floor, getting back in was another story – because the window was about 4 feet off the ground.

I put a stump beneath the window, stepped on it and stepped into the bedroom, showing him how to use it a step.

He looked at me like I was insane.

I put a chair there. Nope. A cement brick-like thing. Nope. I hunched down beneath the window outside, then leapt up like a frog to show him how to hop back inside. Nope. No thank you. No way.

Sigh. Fine. I put my arms beneath his torso and hoisted him up through the window. He bounded in the bedroom, immediately jumped on the bed, gave me the biggest smile a dog could give.

I had apparently passed my first round of training. Oh, the things you do for love.

I got used to Sawyer's quirks. He got used to mine. We agreed on so many things.

Chicken is good. The river is fun. Eating river rocks is not a good idea (which he only learned after an $800 operation to extract one jammed at the top of his intestine).

And we both absolutely loved the beach. The beach in Oregon is not like the beach in Southern California or Florida or anywhere else it's actually hot. The Oregon beach is usually windy and kind of chilly, even in the summer.

All my sundresses and bathing suits were definitely feeling neglected. I didn't wear either one once the entire time I lived in the Pacific Northwest.

As long as you wore a jacket, pants and boots, the craggy, all-natural Oregon beach was a fabulous place. Sawyer and I even found a secret spot we'd drive to every day after work. It was a beach spot blocked off by really tall reeds we had to rustle through to get to the water.

Every day was like a little safari, rustling through the reeds, not being able to see each other. Then we'd finally get to the end of the patch, which opened majestically into a big span of the roiling Pacific Ocean. Ahhh.

Sawyer would make a mad dash for the water, splishing and splashing in the surf. He'd dance on the sand, chase after seagulls. I'd follow behind, bursting with glee. His joy brought on my own joy. I fell harder in love every day.

We typically had the beach to ourselves. Only a fool would want to rustle through those tall reeds to get there. It was as if we were the only two people on earth. Me and Sawyer. Sawyer and me. Our beach romps were magical indeed.

Until the day we found the dead sea lion. I had smelled the rotting sea lion flesh before I saw it, a giant lump of dark-grey-black in the sand. I initially thought it was some type of beached whale – or even a person! But then saw the whiskers when I got a bit closer.

"Let's go the other way," I turned around to tell Sawyer. But it was too late. Once Sawyer had gotten a whiff of that stench, he ran like a bat out of hell toward the oozing, putrefying mass. Then immediately proceeded to roll in it. Not on it. IN it.

He rolled so hard and deep, the edges of the decaying skin draped around him like a coat. I thought of that scene in "Star Wars" when Han Solo cuts open that dead furry taunaun creature and stuffs Luke inside it to keep Luke warm.

Yuck. Double yuck.

"Get the heck outta there!" I yelled at Sawyer. "Get over here!"

I finally had to go pull Sawyer by the collar to get him away from the sea lion. Then pulled him back up the beach, through the reed patch and into the car. The stench was so foul, it permeated my soul – and the car. My eyes began to water. I felt the bile rising in my throat.

I opened all the windows and floored it all the way home, taking Sawyer in the backyard with the hose. It must have taken about five baths to get the stench out of his long, thick fur. And other three days for the car to air out.

I hoisted up the wet and smiling Sawyer from the yard into the bedroom window. He shook off his coat, ran over and hopped up on the bed. He was smiling and panting. No. He was laughing.

Apparently I had passed my second round of training. Oh, the things you do for love.

It's too easy to make a dog your Higher Power, especially when it's a dog named Sawyer.

Rice in the Attic

Hoisting Sawyer in through the bedroom window was getting old. But there was still no way, no how he was going to leave the safety of the bedroom to venture anywhere else in the house. I finally found out why.

It was the same reason he would often stare at the closet, the bedroom door or the hallway and growl. The house was haunted.

One morning I was in the midst of hanging a picture high on the kitchen wall, near the ceiling beneath the attic. I had the ladder. Had the picture. Had the hammer and nails. I positioned one nail where I wanted it, then hit the nail with the hammer.

At the exact moment the nail went into the wall, a ghastly horrific male scream reverberated throughout the house and beyond.

"Ehhhhhhrrrrraaaaaaaaaaaaaaaaaaaaaaaaaaaaaahhhhhhhhhhh hhhhhhhhhhhhhhhhhHHHHHHHHHHHHHHHHHHHHHHHHHH HHHHHHHHHHHHHH"

It was loud, long and terrifying, like someone was being run over with a lawn mower. I ran to the window to look outside. Nothing.

Maybe I had just been imagining it?

I looked at Sawyer. His normally upright, pointy ears were plastered back on his head, like someone took a glue roller to them. Yep. He heard it, too.

The attic was creepy enough to begin with. I went up there once, thinking it might be a good room for a home office setup. There was an old metal bedframe in the middle of the room, reminiscent of the kind you see in abandoned typhoid hospitals.

Nah, I don't want to hang out up here.

I didn't touch anything and went back downstairs.

After the scream, we started hearing footsteps walking back and forth across the attic floor at random hours of the day or night. I tried looking up deaths in that house, but found no record of anything.

I asked the landlords if there had been any murders or suicides in the house, maybe in the attic.

The only answer I got was, "Why do you ask?"

That was confirmation enough for me. Since I didn't have the money or energy to move out, I decided to let the ghost man know we weren't there to disrupt whatever he normally did.

I went up to the attic with a few candles and a bowl of white rice. I said a prayer and told the ghost man we'd just be living downstairs for a while, intending to completely leave him alone. That would be great if he did the same. Oh, and here's some rice as an offering.

Although Sawyer and I still heard footsteps and other weird noises from the attic, and Sawyer continued to stare and growl at the closet, the bedroom door, the hallway, I somehow felt more secure that the ghost man thing wouldn't harm us.

I left the bowl of rice in the attic, even after we moved.

This time I didn't flee the state because of a bad relationship. It was the weather.

The 118 inches of rain per year was really getting me down. Not only did everything smell perpetually musty and soggy, but it was contributing to my depression.

I had used a Happy Light back in New York, where it pretty much stayed grey from November to April. The Happy Light mimicked natural sunlight, and you were supposed to sit in front of it for 10 minutes a day.

To combat all the rain and grey here in the Pacific Northwest, I would need an entire bank of Happy Lights, 25 hours a day. Or maybe even a Happy Light chamber.

All that wiring and special light bulbs would surely get expensive. It seemed more economical to move. So here we go again, this time running from the rain.

I had to go live in a place where it doesn't rain, ever. Tucson, Arizona, was the driest I found, averaging about 12 inches of rain a year – that's a full 106 inches less than I was currently experiencing.

I'm in. Let's do it.

"I knew you wouldn't be staying with us forever," said my Oregon newspaper boss, "but didn't think you'd be moving THIS quick."

I had formed beautiful bonds with several of the people in the office. One even wrote a goodbye song that she sang as she played her guitar for the entire office. I was going to miss these folks for sure.

I initially had no job and no house or apartment lined up, but I was hell-bent on Tucson anyway. Then the magic began to magically unfold.

Some call them coincidences. Others call them God winks. I take them as a sign that I'm doing the right thing, or the thing I'm supposed to be doing to learn, grow and thrive.

And boy, was there a lot of learning that went down in Tucson.

But first I had to get there. So back to the magic unfolding.

It started with an email out of nowhere from someone I had not seen in at least 15 years, since my days with Big John the bouncer in New York City.

Her name was Jennifer and she had been meaning to email me for about a decade now, ever since she saw my byline and email address on a column I had written for a New York City newspaper.

"You might not remember me," but she went on to remind who she was and how she was and how we drank together at Alcatraz. Alcatraz was that bar in Alphabet City that doubled as Big John's main bouncer gig.

She mentioned the night a guy was hitting on us, saying he wanted to steal our underwear, and Big John threw him out of the bar on his head.

It sounded vaguely familiar, and definitely something that Big John would do. He was the protective sort. Guess most bouncers are.

She asked how I was, where I was and how life was going.

"I'm stuck in the rain and need to get out," I told her.

Ended up she owned a house in Tucson, Arizona, which she bought after going to college at the University of Arizona. She lived here for a while, but then was drawn back to New York City.

Someone rented the main house, but the guest house was for rent.

She sent pictures. Sawyer approved. We were sold.

I had the house. Now I needed the job.

That was a bit trickier. I emailed the two newspapers in Tucson, a sweet little note if I say so myself.

"My name is blah blah and here's my experience and I was wondering if you had room on your staff for a creative, dedicated writer?"

One wrote back immediately.

"We have no room."

Geesh. The other said to drop them a line after I moved to town.

I poked around at other publications where writing might be part of the job. An editorial gig at a tourist newspaper sounded promising. The boss man said he'd be glad to give me a go for the editorial position.

Yes!

Got the house. Got the job. Now we just needed to find the nearest dog park. It was within walking distance of the guest house we'd be renting.

Tucson, here we come.

★·····LESSONS LEARNED·····❧

You can often tell how aligned you are with the Universe by how easily solutions unfold. Moving to Tucson was as easy as pecan pie.

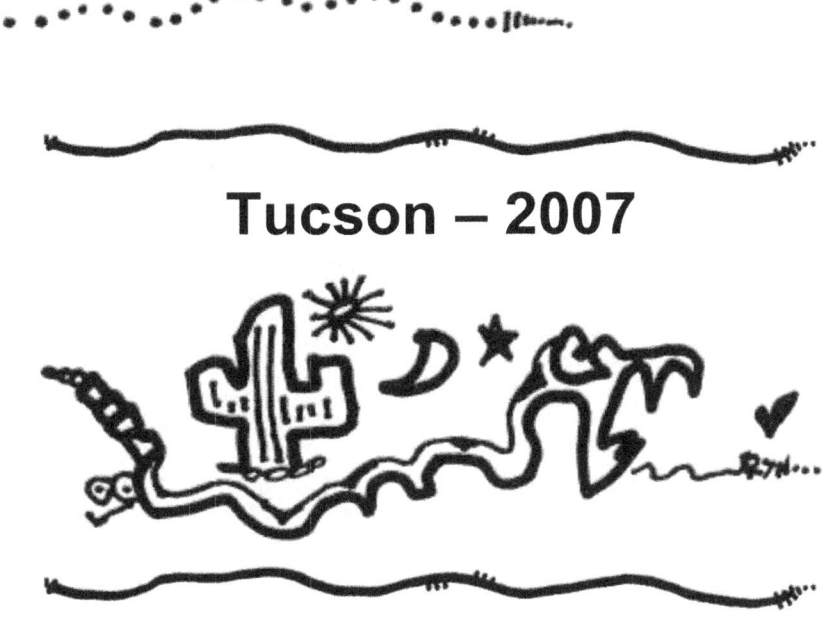

The first thing that struck me about Tucson was that it looked like Mars. At least with just the right sunset.

The whole sky would turn a blood red orange with golden hues, making everything pulsate with an otherworldly glow. I loved it.

Sawyer loved it, too. Instead of hiding in the bedroom like he did in the haunted Oregon farmhouse, he was Mr. King of the House. He took to the desert immediately. Loving the dog park. Loving life.

He even went to get the newspaper for me one day, after it had been thrown over the brick wall fence. He brought it lovingly to my feet, as if someone had trained him to do exactly that.

"What a good boy, thank you!"

He smiled and took in the praise. Then he grabbed the newspaper back and proceeded to shred it.

All was dandy except that job I landed at the tourist newspaper. As promised, the man did hire me. But the job was not about writing at all.

My first day on the job, he plopped a huge phone book in front of me, opened it to a section, and told me to finish that section by lunch.

Do what?

Call each number, one by one, and sell them advertising in our paper.

There were about 500 numbers in the section. Lunch was a 20-minute period that was timed to the millisecond.

You got lunch and two bathroom breaks. The bathroom was outside, around the corner, and in a different little adobe building. Your bathroom breaks were also timed.

If you were not visibly at your desk, time would be taken off your total hours. Oh yeah, and no smoking. At all. Anywhere.

I would suck down a cigarette as fast as I could breathe on the way to the bathroom – then jump up and down thinking the air flow through my clothes would whisk away the smell.

I'd get back to my desk, calling the numbers as fast as I could dial to hit the quota before lunch.

I was hitting the amount of calls I was supposed to make, but on the third day he threatened to fire me anyway.

"You haven't sold a single ad," he said. "This is not the kind of performance I can tolerate. It's lack of performance."

I went back to my desk, vowing to do better, wondering how you were supposed to sell something you didn't want to sell and no one wanted to buy.

I felt stuck. Abused, Disgusted. Mad at myself for being tricked. Mad at myself for not being able to quit. I needed a job. I needed the money. I was cemented in this hell hole by fear.

And even if it was like being an indentured servant, at least I didn't have to flip hamburgers or file insurance papers. Actually, filing insurance papers was a dream job compared to this.

I'd get home and cry every day. Sometimes I didn't wait until I got home. I'd cry at my desk, hiding my tears behind the big fat phonebook.

Other employees would come out of boss man's office, also crying. It seemed the workplace where anger, fear and tears were the norm.

Sawyer was my comfort, even if he did chew up the newspaper. I also had the fledgling hope that the other newspaper would finally grant me an interview, hire me, take me away from this pit of abuse.

Then one day, it happened.

First the interview. Then the feedback. "I like you. You seem scrappy." Then the wait for the final decision. Then the big, happy "Yes!"

Yes, they had room on their staff. I would start two weeks from Sunday, the evening crime shift.

Glee exploded through my veins. I couldn't wait to tell make-them-cry boss man that I quit, I quit, I quit!

Glee was tempered by fear when it came time to head into his office and break the news. He didn't take it well. I was the most ungrateful person he ever met. He had fulfilled his promise of giving me a job, and this is how I thank him?!

I felt about two inches tall and shrinking fast during his lashing.

"I need to take this opportunity," I told him. "I was hoping you wouldn't hate me."

"Hate you?" he retorted. "You're not worth the energy."

The door slammed behind me as I skittered out of his office. I grabbed my purse from my desk. Said goodbye and good luck to the two other tear-soaked employees. And did a happy dance all the way home.

The Tucson newspaper job was heaven.

And the crime beat. Oh, the beloved crime beat. True crime writer Ann Rule was at the top of my idol list, right along with my other writing heroes: Shel Silverstein; Erma Bombeck; Charles Baudelaire; Charles Bukowski.

Ann Rule had actually known Ted Bundy when he was a working on a suicide hotline. Like others who knew and liked him, she had been floored when the world learned he was a serial killer.

While there weren't any serial killers in Tucson during my newspaper days, or at least any that we knew of, there were plenty of other crimes.

My training as an alcoholic was perfect for the beat. Years of drinking had numbed me, shut off all emotions.

Heck, I wasn't even ticklish anymore. I was able to turn off emotions in a heartbeat, cover stories that would make most people sick enough to go home for a week.

The annual obituary roundup was another project where my emotional shutdown was an asset. This involved a story featuring 12 Tucsonans who had died over the past year, one for each month.

It also involved lengthy phone calls to family members and friends, who would now be facing their first Christmas and New Year without their beloved. Sometimes the calls were very lengthy. But that was OK.

They always thanked me for listening, for paying tribute to their loved ones. They shared stories and laughter and moments of glee.

I knew I was losing the 10-foot wall around me when I hung up the phone after one of those calls and there were actually tears in my eyes.

Dammit. I was softening.

I hoped no one had seen, then grabbed the next grisly lead to get back into the crime mindset.

Opening my heart made me feel vulnerable. If I kept up that 10-foot wall, I was much more secure. No feelings go in. No feelings go out. Just a stone face like those Mount Rushmore things – but hopefully a bit more attractive.

When I wasn't covering crime, I was the designated general reporter. That meant I covered anything and everything that didn't fit neatly into one of the other boxes. Oh yeah, I also got the animal beat.

Perhaps the 32 framed photos of Sawyer all around my desk gave them a hint I was an animal lover. Especially dogs. Especially Sawyer.

Such joy to share the antics of Sawyer with my other dog-loving coworkers. Or anyone who would listen, actually. Sawyer my soul mate dog. He did this. He did the other thing. One day he's going to write his own blog!

My coworkers were cool enough about my worship of Sawyer, as some loved dogs as much as I loved Sawyer. Well, maybe not THAT much.

That is, of course, except one. There's always got to be that one. It was the new managing editor who was hired the same day I was. He ambled over one day when I was gushing about Sawyer and asked a question.

"What are you going to do when that dog dies?"

I disliked him immediately.

.....LESSONS LEARNED......

Everything in the desert is armed, ready to hurt you if you mess with it. No wonder I loved it so much. I could definitely relate.

A Growing Family

Me and Sawyer, Sawyer and me. I lived my life around that dog. I'd plan my vacations around him. Got him a sister to pal around with while I was working. She was a barky dog named Dini. When I was scoping out dogs at the rescue shelter, Sawyer ignored them all except this one.

Dini came out to play and did ninja jumps back and forth over Sawyer's back. Then they both ran over to the little outside fountain and broke the lever that regulated the water flow.

The perfect pair! We'll take her.

It was only later I learned she had been given back to the shelter at least three or four times from others who tried to adopt her. Two said they had cats in the household and Dini positively hated cats. She'd try to eat them.

Others had said she just wouldn't stop barking. But she came with free obedience lessons. We attended them dutifully. She passed!

Only one Tucson neighbor ended up moving due to the incessant barking, on and on. Without those lessons, it may have been three or four, right?

We also had to "disown" her once at the beach. On our twice-yearly trip to San Diego's dog beach, Dini would stand by the shoreline and bark, bark, bark, bark for however long we hung out there.

Wouldn't seem to be barking at anything. Wouldn't stop for nothing.

She was far enough away from our beach setup that we could keep an eye on her without it being obvious she belonged to us. Every person who walked by would be stymied by the chunky black dog that stood there, barking at nothing.

"Whose dog is that?" they'd ask us.

"We have no idea."

While you may have assumed the "we" was referring to me and Sawyer, there was actually another soul in the picture by now. His name was Robert and we met online. Not on a dating site, but on the newspaper website.

It was back in the day when it was a big thing for newspapers to go online, and the Tucson Citizen made the leap into having both a print and online edition. In those early online days, we were so young and innocent.

The publisher left the comments open. And readers actually left meaningful comments on the stories.

We ended up with a little group of commenters who had tons of fun bantering back and forth. We'd joke around, share thoughts and ideas. Have good-natured debates. One guy with a skull avatar would consistently show up to make comments on my columns. His comments were sarcastic and weird.

I was falling in love.

We finally met in person when he bought some of my art. A custom metal sign for his condo porch. He wanted a brown and purple polka-dot gecko named Gertie.

He was coming to my house to pick up the art. He asked if it was OK to bring his daughter. Sure, I said.

But inside, I was already recoiling. Oh no, not this kid thing again. My thoughts shot right back to New Mexico. Here comes another surly teen that's going smoke in the house and be punished by raking up goat poop.

I opened the door to see the most adorable 7-year-old little girl. And a guy who looked…well, normal.

You gotta love when your mind automatically makes things horrific. There's even a word for it: catastrophizing. In any case, I'm glad she wasn't a surly teen since I didn't have any goat poop in the yard for her to rake.

I wasn't allowed to have goats where I lived in Tucson (I had already checked).

Robert and I started emailing daily. Our relationship grew from there. He was hitting all the right points. He was sarcastic and funny. He laughed at my jokes. His kid wasn't a surly teen. He bought my art. What more do you need in a man?

It ends up there was one more thing. He was already married.

He dropped the married bombshell as he was about to ask me on our first date, telling me there was something I needed to know.

Wow. I'd say.

The married thing was a shocker for sure. But just as I was about to fall off the cliff into another pity pot about always picking the wrong guys, he filled me in on the rest of the story.

He was married, yes. Technically. But they had been separated for years. He lived alone in his own condo, got his daughter on whatever schedule. The relationship was over, he insisted.

"Then why aren't you divorced?"

No one ever bothered to file the paperwork, he explained. He figured he was done with relationships so he had no reason to. Who wants to go through all the hassle and expense when you can just let a dead relationship linger, turning black and rancid on the vine.

Well, he didn't put it like that. But you get the idea. And so did I. I immediately thought of Morty and how our relationship had been dead for years before I finally got the courage to move out.

Sometimes it's just easier to live in misery than to make a big scary change. Humans typically need a great motivation to change. Like waiting until you're actually on your deathbed before you quit drinking. Or having a newspaper reporter columnist artist gal tell you she won't date you until you get a divorce.

Within a week he showed up beaming, waving copies of his official divorce papers.

Never mind dinner and the movies. Our first date was a picnic in Arivaca. Arivaca is not far from Tucson. It's one of those unincorporated areas that you want to call a city but it's really not.

It had a lake and lots of ramshackle abandoned houses. I insisted we explore the houses. Robert spent the whole time telling me to watch where I stepped and how the ceiling could come crashing down any minute and crush my head.

Didn't he know he was talking to someone who used to live in places that were worse?

No, I guess he didn't. He didn't know all that much about me, nor me about him. I had yet to have the "big talk," that scary early dating moment when you tell the other person you're an alcoholic.

Telling someone early on had become my M.O., just to get it out in the open. In one of my previous relationships, I hadn't mentioned until we had been dating for a bit. The guy ended up getting really weird after the news, sneaking rum and cokes while we were watching movies. Then ghosting me.

When I finally got him to talk to tell me why, he said he couldn't envision living his whole life without drinking.

Oh. I didn't know we were getting married.

The break-up ached at first, but then I realized I was better off without someone like that.

Then it became good riddance. No great loss. Especially since he was the same guy who said I had to see this absolutely hilarious video he had – and then played a Claymation mini-movie of people pooping on each other.

Robert was different. He didn't think Claymation poop was hilarious. Or at least I hoped he didn't. And our first date in Arivaca was going great. Until he pulled out a 10-inch knife.

Yeah, I was taken aback for sure. I figured that was the end of me, out here in unincorporated boonies, a scant 11 miles from the Mexican border. I pictured chunks of my chopped-up body strewn across the desert landscape, being picked at by vultures and coyotes.

But the knife, it was all he had, sorry. It was a hunting knife he kept his truck. He meant to bring a smaller kitchen knife to cut our sandwiches and pickles.

We ate merrily by the lake, fending off gnats and looking at some strange webbed cocoons in the tree branches that we were sure must have come from outer space.

By the time we were done hanging out in the heat by the lake, securing my abandoned-house finds in his pickup and finally heading home, we both reeked of B.O. It made the whole truck stink. But neither of us cared one bit. Oh, isn't new love just dreamy?

The relationship was moving smoothly. And it scared the hell out of me. One pocket of fear stemmed from the idea that all good things come to an end. So I might as well sit around being afraid of the end.

The other pocket of fear came from the fact that Robert was unlike anyone I had previously dated. He was kind. Respectful. Considerate. Didn't move in with me after the first week of dating. The whole situation was throwing me for a loop. I was almost scared enough to break it off just because it freaked me out so much.

He didn't even care about the alcoholic thing, which I disclosed to him during our third date while we were sitting in the dark in front of eegee's eating lemon slushies. (I had never heard of eegee's either. It's a Tucson and Phoenix thing, a fast food joint with the best slushies.)

Not only did Robert not care about the alcoholism, but he disclosed he had some issues with drinking in the past. A big, ugly DUI charge that came with aggravated assault. They claimed he was using his vehicle as a weapon.

Suddenly I felt better.

Whew. OK. He does have some craziness in his background. God forbid I should be dating Beaver Cleaver!

But that craziness was done now. He had stopped drinking on his own. He could take it or leave it. And if it made me uncomfortable, he had no problem leaving it.

I tried to poke and prod and pick and examine and geesh, I couldn't find anything wrong with him. Even Sawyer liked him, the dog who trusted no one. It had to be the first healthy relationship I had been in, ever, and it was freaking me out.

Even freakier, I had told him about the 10-foot wall around my heart that kept all emotions and intimacy as far away as Arivaca. He said, if I wanted, he would make it his mission to help me tear it down.

Talk about a glee train. I was on it. When I was first moving to Tucson, one of my poet pals from back in Brooklyn sent me a postcard that said: "You will love Tucson, and Tucson will love you."

Man, I was feeling the love. Robert and I were getting closer. My parents loaned me money to buy a Tucson home of my own. The newspaper job was rocking. I had found my calling. I loved my coworkers. I loved my bosses.

I loved winning awards for my column and reporting – including Best Feature Column in Arizona. I even loved those little certificates I kept getting at the staff meetings for being employee of the month. I loved most everything about my job.

Heck, it was more than a job. It was a career. At age 38, I finally had a career!

The desert was magical. My house was phenomenal. My relationship was fabulous. And I could work at the paper forever and ever until I was old enough to retire and paint skulls in the desert.

Yes, I had found my stride. Found my bliss. Found the work and place I want to stick with for the rest of my life.

And then, a millisecond later, it all came crashing down.

✱.....LESSONS LEARNEd......℮

When life is good, it can be very, very good. But when it is bad, it gets horrid.

End of an Era

Originally called the Arizona Citizen and established in 1870, the Tucson Citizen newspaper where I worked was the oldest in the state. We had a strong staff of amazing journalists, back in the day when stories were actually researched, factual, balanced and fair.

We weren't even allowed to put political bumper stickers on our cars or signs in our yards. Opinions were saved for the editorial pages.

Every story had to have at least two or three sources, and those sources had to be named. And no, random tweets and recycled Facebook posts from God-knows-where didn't count.

It was a paper backed by talent, integrity, blood, sweat and love. And it was all reduced to tears the day the man in the suit came. The man in the suit was a bigwig from Gannett, which had owned the paper since 1976.

We were all called into the lobby area to listen to this man who told us three things.

"The paper is making money, but not enough money." That was thing number one.

"So we're closing it down." Thing number two.

Thing number three put the icing on the cake.

"I have a reservation to go golfing so I have to leave."

With that, he was gone. With that, my whole career was gone. The other newspaper in Tucson was already fully staffed. No matter what kind of writing-related job I applied to, I'd be competing against dozens of other out-of-work journalists who were so unkindly left to rot in the streets.

The real estate market had just crashed, so my mortgage was now higher than my Tucson home was worth.

I couldn't sell and run, which was my first inclination. Maybe I could rent it out and run? Maybe I could just run?

That booming message from an early sponsor echoed through my head.

"One day you'll realize, Ryn, there is nowhere left to run."

I wanted to weep. So I did.

Those last three months at the newspaper were hell. Even though we all knew we'd be out of a job come March, we were supposed to keep the paper up and running until then. Sure, we could quit. But everyone was hanging on to that last shard of a paycheck until they got another job.

Giant garbage and recycling collection bins were in the middle of the newsroom, with more stuff being piled in them every day. The chatter was hollow. The laugher was gone. No more debates about this, that and the other intriguing thing.

The only debate I recall was whether to put a yellow bicycle helmet that nobody wanted in the bin for recycling or garbage. The helmet went from one bin to the other, back and forth, until someone got fed up and threw it in the parking lot.
That pretty much summed it all up.

That was the work front. On the home front, there was no way I could make the mortgage payments without my full-time job. I had been freelancing on the side, but that was only a few hours a week.

Gannett had decided to keep the online version of the paper alive, but in a different capacity. It would be a blog site, with blogs written by people in the community, for free. And they would keep two employees who would write their own blogs and run the thing. They needed an editor and a writer.

For the writer, they picked me! It was a welcome relief that I'd still have a job, but I immediately felt guilty that all my coworkers would not. Except for the editor they chose to be my boss.

So guess who? That's right. The managing editor who, when we first met, had made that crack about what was I going to do when Sawyer died.

I wanted to puke. He walked over and started chatting about the schedule, as if we had been pals forever. It still amazes me how the people you resent often have no clue that just looking at them makes your blood curdle.

"Resentment is like drinking poison and waiting for the other person to die."

I think Carrie Fisher said that. Or Saint Augustine. Ironically, Carrie Fisher forever resented her role as Princess Leia in "Star Wars." Said it ruined her life.

In any event, I was drinking poison. And managing editor man was still standing there, chatting and smiling, without the faintest clue.

The blogsite job was actually a welcome relief. I started having fun with it. I was allowed to work from home. I could still pay my mortgage. And I even talked managing editor into Sawyer getting his own blog, "Sawyer Says." It was all about pets and animals.

I ended up writing three blog posts a day, finishing by early afternoon, and grabbing freelance work on the side. Yeah, this was OK. I could hack it. Although going to the office was a total nightmare.

Just walking up through the parking lot was depressing, since we were still in the same building where the paper was once alive. The huge newsroom stood empty. We were instead crammed into a little office off to the side. It had no windows and concrete walls.

You could feel the sadness every time you walked in the doors, especially when you knew the other paper was bustling away in all its glory in the very same building. They were even stronger now, with no competition.

But thankfully I only had to go into the office once in a while for whatever special reason. Or at least that was the case for the first year, until managing editor decided to switch things up.

"I'm sick of running the blog site," he said. "Starting in January, you're going to be the new site administrator. So forget about writing your three blogs, or writing anything. You'll be handling all the technical stuff and working out of the office five days a week."

My mouth said nothing. My head said "Kiss my foot!"

I went home to mull it over. Fear told me to stay and keep getting that paycheck. My soul said to break free, that the new role would kill me.

For one of the few times in my life, fear lost. I broke free about a month before I was supposed to start the new position. And I did it in a way that made me feel so good, at least at the time.

Managing editor said since I was on salary, I would be required to work whatever hours were needed with no extra pay. And we're going to start now, a Saturday in December, since he needed me to come in and help him train the new gaggle of bloggers.

This was before I had decided to set my soul free and was still counting on the job and the paycheck. So I said I'd be there. Then went home and cried.

My woe soon turned to anger. Then to rage.

I talked it over with my then-sponsor and we concocted the most fantastic idea.

Instead of showing up for work on Saturday, I would instead deliver my resignation letter. But instead of showing up to hand it to managing editor in person, I would post it online on my blog.

The letter didn't attack him or say anything I could be arrested for, but it was very strong. It also outlined how I had felt about being demoted from a creative force to an administrative robot. It wasn't very nice.

I posted it that morning, started getting comments immediately.

"Good for you, Ryn!"

"You tell 'em!"

"I'm with you, girl!"

"Don't waste your talents in administrative work. I love your writing!"

There were dozens of comments by early afternoon. Then, in a flash, it was gone. The post was gone. My whole blog was gone. All three of my blogs were gone, including Sawyer's.

I was deleted from the entire website with a whoosh, as if I had never existed.

I had a feeling all my posts would be deleted. I had prepared.

Delete all you want, mister man, as I had already downloaded and backed-up all the blog posts before that morning. So there!

The adrenaline rush of doing something really daring stuck with me for a few weeks. Until I started to feel guilty about it. Damn Catholic upbringing. Guilt is woven into the fabric of being. That's why hair shirts and self-flagellation was invented.

Just thinking about them made my back hurt and my skin itch.

I knew I'd have to eventually make amends for my actions to the managing editor. The word "eventually" was the key here. In the meantime, I was too busy wondering where the heck my next paycheck would come from, or how I would afford the mortgage.

For the paycheck, I started doing what I always did when afraid. I zoomed into a knee-jerk reaction where I started applying for any and every job within a 50-mile radius, whether I wanted to work there or not.

I got exactly one interview out of the flurry. I don't even remember the publication, except that the topics sounded about as exciting as spending a week in a locked room. They granted me a phone interview.

After telling me there were about 10 other former Tucson Citizen staff members applying for this single position, they asked a series of questions involving real-life scenarios.

One was what I would do if I was working with a designer creating a project and the designer and I disagreed on what the final product should look like.

I don't recall my exact words, but I do remember the gist of my response. I basically said I would let the designer have their way, for they were mightier and more experienced and I'm just a spineless worm who doesn't know anything about design.

They never called me back.

I later realized what I said was also untrue on various levels.

The same way it's a bad idea to go grocery shopping when you're hungry, it's an even worse idea to answer interview questions when your self-confidence is at negative 300.

Unless, of course, the employer is specifically seeking out a spineless worm.

But there was likely another element at play, that fun thing called the subconscious. We can push our consciousness to align with what the head is telling us to do, but the subconscious is where our deepest desires live.

As I became more self-aware, I was noticing how my subconscious would have its way by coming out sideways.

No, I didn't want that boring publication job. But I made myself apply for it because it would give me a steady income and seemed the logical thing to do. My subconscious, on the other hand, was screaming to screw logic. And definitely screw that job.

It then helped me answer the question in the most horrendous way to automatically take me out of the running. On the conscious level, I could say I tried. It's not my fault they didn't want a spineless worm.

On the subconscious level I could breathe a sigh of much-needed and much-warranted relief. And do it. Finally do it. Finally pursue my REAL dream job.

...Lessons Learned...

God does for us what we cannot do for ourselves. I was never going to quit the newspaper job, no matter how much I dreamed of being my own boss one day. God must have decided the own-boss dream needed to come true.

Birth of a Dream

For years I had yearned to be my own boss. Set my own hours. Work when I wanted, on what I wanted. Be a freelance writer galore!

I had been freelancing part-time for years. With no feasible job I wanted in Tucson and no way to move, this would be the perfect time to push it into full-time. Even my conscious mind was agreeing. This was good.

It was also tough. My first move was to get an art shop going online, so I could be a freelance writer AND artist galore. I was experimenting with metal art, specifically metal signs cut in the shape of animals and painted in fun funky colors.

My Beware of Dog signs soon became and remained my best seller.

Doubling down on the freelance writing assignments was my second move. I grabbed at any and all assignments I could find on a host of different freelance writing websites. I calculated how much I wanted to make every week, and then crammed X number of assignments into my schedule to make it happen.

I was working double time. Triple time. And sometimes on topics that made me want to scream.

Other topics were just plain dumb. One now-defunct writing site offered an array of how-to articles that paid $25 a pop. One topic I picked was "How to Tame a Lion."

I thought it would be all in fun, but it came back with a legion of edits – as if the average reader on this general how-to site would use this article to ace a career in lion taming.

Whatever. The articles were pretty easy to write, letting me make my quota. But the editors on the site were like those mid-level managers that need to create something to do to validate their jobs. The articles would come back with the most ridiculous edits, finding issues where there were none.

Sigh. I knew it was over when an article about fun places to visit in New York City came back.

"Brooklyn is not in New York City. Please revise."

I lived there for 17 years, you dolt. Please go fly a kite.

OK, I didn't write that. But I thought it. And I did indignantly attach a little map of the five boroughs of New York City to my response that told the editor Coney Island was fun and why don't they go there to walk off a pier if they don't believe me.

Yes, that gig was over.

But again, what seemed like the end of the world was just the beginning of something beautifully better. I found new websites and new clients. Clients that adored my work. Clients that paid me better than $25 a pop.

Clients that wouldn't send things back with idiot edits. Well, I still had some of those. I think writers will always get some of those.

My writing career grew. It blossomed. I wrote some fun books. My artwork was selling in dribs and drabs.

I was making enough to live on, but there was still the mortgage issue.

When I knew the newspaper gig was truly over, I contacted the bank for what's called a mortgage modification. That means they adjust your monthly payments to a lower level so you can afford them, usually by stretching out the length of your loan.

I remember using frou-frou terms like "financial hardship" and "loan restructuring" in my very professional letter to the bank.

No response.

Sent the letter again the next month. Then the next.

Still no response.

I asked a realtor friend what was going on, why wasn't the bank responding.

"Are you still making your monthly payments?" she asked. I was.

"That's why. Stop paying them."

Wha?!

It ends up the banks won't even consider a modification unless you're falling behind on your payments. Why should they? You can't cry financial hardship and then keep sending them money. Or at least that's the way the system works.

No, I couldn't afford the current payments, but I thought I could just have a pleasant conversation with the bank and they'd give me a break. [Insert laughter here.]

The idea of not making the monthly payments made me feel slimy. Like a ne'er-do-well or a liar. I had signed on the dotted line, promising to pay. And now I wouldn't?

And what then? What if the bank didn't grant a modification? What if the house goes into foreclosure?

Tons of foreclosures were happening right about then, thanks to the real estate market crash and the previous practices of giving anyone and everyone a loan – even if they made about five cents a year.

This foreclosure thing was scary. I'd lose the deposit my parents loaned me. They'd kill me! I'd lose the years' worth of mortgage payments I already sunk into the house.

Even worse, I'd have nowhere to live. I'd have to go live under a dusty underpass in the searing Tucson heat!

All this, and I hadn't even stopped paying the mortgage yet. Imagine what my head was like when I actually did follow the realtor's suggestion and stop making the payments.

Let's just say it was a year of hell.

Every month, the payment due date would come and go. Every month, I would send the same letter asking for a loan modification.

The bank waited until I was several months behind on payments before responding. They did so in the form of nasty calls from loan collectors. And I mean nasty.

One woman yelled at me for so hard and so long I was actually crying when I hung up the phone.

Bank paperwork finally came filtering in. They wanted proof of financial hardship. I had to gather up about 52 different documents and send them their way.

The next month, the same thing. More nasty phone calls. More paperwork. The paperwork I sent last month was now outdated. I needed to send a new batch reflecting activity for the past 30 days.

This went on. And on. And on. For about a year. Then came the big notice I had been dreading from the start:

FORECLOSURE.

My house was about five minutes away from foreclosure unless I paid all the past-due monies I owed or came to an agreement with the bank. How could I come to an agreement with the bank if I was never offered an agreement from the bank?!

Where were we going to live?

Robert was living with me at this point, but he still owned his condo. He was currently renting it. The second-floor, one-bedroom unit was the perfect place for a single guy. Not so perfect for two people and two big dogs who didn't like going up and down the stairs.

What will we do? How will I ever make back all that money I lost, the deposit, the payments?

I cussed the realtor to the ends of the universe and back for her suggestion. Then cussed myself even harder for following it.

We were about one minute away from foreclosure when the bank sent a modification agreement. It was the worst agreement you could devise, with a massive balloon payment encompassing all the past due monies and all the extra monies they were shaving off the monthly payments going forward for the next 22 years.

That balloon payment amount had already racked up tons of interest payments on top of the initial amount, and it would continue to do so until the end of time. But yes, the monthly payments were less. And by that point I didn't have much choice but to take it.

"Check here to agree to the new terms of the loan. Check here to reject the modification and move forward with foreclosure proceedings."

As crummy as the deal was, at least that year of anguish was over. I had been functioning during that year, but it was with a huge knot in my stomach every single day.

I had also started working with a new sponsor. She was amazing. Not only was she funny and smart, but her career was in behavioral health.

Yes! A shrink and a sponsor wrapped in one.

We met every week. It was the first time someone actually took me through the Big Book proper. All other sponsors told me to make sure I read it, or never mentioned it at all. That book is has been a notable component in my growth, as were our discussions and the sponsor's invaluable direction.

While I had been in recovery for more than 10 years at this point, I wasn't free of so many things. I could see that back in New Mexico I was actually what they call a "dry drunk," or exhibiting the same actions a drinker would have – just without the alcohol.

Why the heck else would I have even considered having a relationship with Mr. New Mexico? Geesh. The dry drunkness followed me around for years. It was time to go deeper to gut out the garbage, deeper than I had ever gone before.

I still had a load of fears and resentments, along with low self-esteem, guilt, shame, massive mistrust and a mean streak of jealousy I just couldn't shake.

"You don't trust others because you don't trust yourself," my new sponsor-shrink told me. "You think other people are going to act the same way you did when you were drinking. They're not you. And you're no longer drinking."

When I first started working with that sponsor, I was actually still afraid to visit my parents. This was after my big rounds of amends had already been done years and years ago. There were still deeper issues that needed to be resolved. Like how I felt my mom nagged me about this, that and the other thing.

"She doesn't sound like a nagging mother," sponsor-shrink said. "She sounds like a mother who has your best interests in mind, who doesn't want you to get hurt."

Whoa.

"If you want self-esteem, do esteem-able things."

Double whoa.

"Don't walk and chew gum at the same time."

Just kidding on that last one. But you get the idea.

We even set up a two-minute rule. If I was sitting and stewing in any emotions or situations for more than two minutes, I was to give her a call.

Of course, I usually didn't. The phone tends to get big, heavy and even scary when you have to pick it up to ask for help. But when I did call, it was miraculous how the stress, tension or anger would gush out of me like a rushing stream.

Talking about things brings relief, just like a fortune cookie once told me:

"Joy shared is doubled. Sorrow shared is halved."

So what do you do with the other half of sorrow that's left? Give it to God.

★....LESSONS LEARNED.....℮

Life is one big rollercoaster. You can hold on with a death-grip and pray for it to stop. Or you stop attempting to control it, then sit back and enjoy the ride.

Broken

As I was getting more into the practices of living a spiritual life, the brighter and better life became. I had been meditating since early sobriety, but I no longer did it crouched beneath a kitchen table next to a cat box.

That helped. A lot. So did opening my eyes and mind to the miracles, joy and love all around me. Especially the love I shared with Sawyer.

My bond with the big, lovable oaf of a dog had gotten even deeper. Dini was also in the picture, of course, still playing the dutiful second fiddle. I loved her as a dog OK, but I didn't share the same profound connection that I did with Sawyer.

Sawyer was my soul mate dog. He was my rock. He was my constant companion. He was my main source of happiness on this earthly plane. I made him my all and everything. I turned him into my higher power.

How could I not? We went through so much together. The haunted farm house in Oregon. The big move to Arizona. Opening our arms (and paws) to Robert. The job loss. The foreclosure BS. Now all was smooth and sweet.

Until the day Sawyer came home from an evening walk, plopped down on the living room floor, and never stood up again.

At first we thought he might just be tired from the walk. Or at least we wished that. Sawyer was only 8 years old. I knew in my heart something was wrong. Really, really wrong.

Ends up he had lost function of the entire back half of his body. His back legs no longer worked. He could no longer control his bladder.

The dog we dubbed "The Bubble" was now miserable and about as non-bubbly as you could get. His eyes were flat and filled with sorrow.

Robert called his sister, who brought her adult son. It took four of us to lift up the blanket on which I had placed him to get him into the back of an SUV to take him to the vet.

The vet ran tests. And more tests. And then a series of other tests. They could find nothing wrong. They could dive deeper into the issue with an MRI. But the only MRI machine for animals in the region was in Phoenix, about 128 miles away.

Someone would have to drive Sawyer there. The MRI cost $1,100.

And there was no guarantee they'd find what was wrong. Even if they did, there was no guarantee it could be something that could be fixed. The ball was in my court. What did I want to do?

I wanted to save him at all costs. I hopped online and bought a doggie wheelchair. I started planning out the physical therapy treatments in my head.

"Ryn, he's 128 pounds. We couldn't even get the wheelchair through the back door to get him out to the yard. How are we going to lift him on our own every time he needs to move?"

Robert was the voice of reason, and I hated him for it.

There was no reasoning. There was only blind determination.

I will save Sawyer. I will save Sawyer. Sawyer cannot and will not die.

When we went to visit Sawyer at the vet the next day, he was actually smiling again. They had cleaned him up, put him on an IV for hydration, gave him painkillers for the agony.

"Look, he's all happy again," I told Robert.

"Don't forget he's on painkillers. He still can't walk."

Dammit. Dammit. Dammit. Why can't he just be miraculously fixed?

Planning and scheduling the big long Phoenix trip would take some time. Sawyer would need to stay at the Tucson vet while this was going on. There was no way we could properly care for him at home at this point.

The ball was still my court. The vet bills were mounting. I would pay any amount to save my soul mate dog – but there was no way to know if he'd ever get better. From what he vet had told after I begged her for direction, the chances of any type of recovery were excruciatingly slim. In fact, she had never seen a recovery from this type of issue.

"This is the point," she said softly, "that most owners say goodbye."

No. No. NO. Sawyer cannot and WILL NOT DIE.

I called my parents for their input. No one was giving me an answer I liked, so I had to keep trying. I was sobbing so hard when they answered the phone, I began spewing gobbledygook.

"What's the matter?" they asked. "What's going on? We can't even understand what you're saying."

I relayed the whole sad story update. Asked them what I should do.

Dad gave me an answer that spoke directly to my heart.

"If I was a dog that used to run and play and I was in constant pain and could no longer run and play, I wouldn't want to live."

His answer was about much more than giving me direction on Sawyer. It was paralleling his own life. Since his retirement a small handful of years ago, Dad had been on his own health decline.

Massive back agony. Acute pain throughout the rest of his body on a daily basis. He had undergone something like 13 different operations.

The first one was the only one that had brought at least a smidgeon of relief. The rest only seemed to make things worse. His lineup of daily pills took up all the room in the cupboard.

Doctors had no clue on the cause of it all.

The man who had been a football superstar in college, until he was foiled by blood clots, was now walking with a cane. Pain was eating him from the inside out. Every time I saw him, he was smaller, more stooped, and weaker. My once giant man dad was becoming a shrinking shell.

Dad wasn't just talking about Sawyer. He was talking about himself.

I put myself in their shoes. Dad, a size 13. Sawyer with his giant paws. Giant paws that would probably never again romp through the desert, give me five with a smile, or hop on my bed to hog it in luxury.

No, I wouldn't want to live either.

Trying to keep Sawyer alive was something I was doing for me, not necessarily for him.

What kind of quality of life could he ever again have?

I told the vet we could move forward with the goodbye. It was one of the toughest decisions I ever made.

*·····LESSONS LEARNED·····℮

As much as losing Sawyer was going to hurt, it hurt even worse when I refused to accept it. Living in denial is painful and delusional – but sometimes we still to do it in the hopes of avoiding the inevitable.

Shattered

The vet had a special consultation room reserved for moments like these. The worst moments of your life. It was a cushy room with carpet and couches and a warm ambiance – not the tile and stark white walls of the other rooms at the vet.

When Robert and I entered, Sawyer was already there, smiling and laying on a blanket in the middle of the room. I sat down next to him. Caressed his head. Looked into his eyes. Told him how much I loved him so, more than anything I had ever loved before.

He looked at me and smiled that Bubble smile.

The vet came in. Sat down on the floor across from us. She had the syringe ready. First he would drift off to sleep. Then the second component would kick in and Sawyer's heart would stop.

She injected him. Sawyer got drowsy. He was still smiling as he softly lowered his head, laid it on my thigh.

"He knows who he belongs to," said the vet.

Yes. I belonged to him. He belonged to me.

I kept caressing his head as his eyes closed. I kept caressing his head as he stopped breathing.

The vet checked his heart with her stethoscope. She looked up at me, made eye contact.

"He's gone."

"NOOOOOOOOOOOOOOOOOOOOOOOOOOOOooo!!!!!!!!!!!!!!!!!!!!!!!!!!!!!!!!!!"

A guttural scream erupted from my soul. I'm pretty sure it shook the walls of the cushy little vet room. I kept screaming all the way back to the car. I kept screaming as Robert drove us home.

I kept screaming and screaming and knew I couldn't stay in the house. Everything in the house reminded me of Sawyer. I had to get out of there. Thankfully, I didn't want to go drink. But I did want to go die. I did what I had trained myself to do over the past 15 years.

My car drove itself to a recovery meeting.

I could barely see the road through my tears. But I did see an answer to my prayer.

"Please God, please God, please God! Give me a sign that Sawyer went to heaven!"

I looked up, and there it was. Directly above me in a clear blue sky was a giant puffy Sawyer-shaped cloud.

God gave me a Sawyer-shaped cloud. God gave me a Sawyer-shaped cloud.

The screaming didn't stop for weeks. I had never known such pain. It felt like a giant spike was being driven through the center of my heart, through the center of my soul, through the center of every fiber of my entire being.

My most vivid recollection of that early mourning period is lying on the living room couch and writhing in anguish. Writhing like I did on the floor all those years ago in my Brooklyn apartment.

But this time it was even more painful. And instead of a voice telling me that maybe there is no God, I had to accept the fact that my dog God was gone.

It wasn't just the grief of losing Sawyer that was hitting me, either. It was a volcano of grief related to all the situations in the past where I refused to deal with the grief, the times I stuffed it down or drank it away.

It never really goes away. It just festers and waits. Waits until a fault line cracks. Sawyer's death was the fault line.

My grief was Mount Saint Helen erupting.

I had no idea what to do, how to handle it, what these horrible feelings were coursing through my veins. I just knew I wanted to die. I wanted to die to escape. I wanted to be free of these feelings.

I screamed and screamed and screamed.

Robert suggested I go back to therapy.

I loved the therapist immediately. I loved her even more when her suggestions helped and soothed me. The book "Good Grief" was a massive help. It's short. It's easy to read, even through tear-streaked eyeballs. It walks you through the stage of grief.

Every time I felt like I was losing my mind, it was comforting to find a description of what I was going through. I wasn't losing my mind after all, it says this is expected, right here, on page 83.

Processing all that grief took some time. A lot of time. I learned a litany of valuable lessons – like not to make your dog your higher power. It was time to give that role back to God.

And not to rely on a Sawyer, a person, a new pair of shoes or other outside force for my happiness. Robert dodged a bullet with that one, as I had been ready to automatically shift him into the role of being my sole source of happiness.

Happiness doesn't come from some outside force. It comes from inside. It's a byproduct of living a life that makes you happy.

I also learned how I was still closing people out, despite opening up my heart fully to Sawyer. I was even keeping Robert at bay, in his own little circle, over there. I learned how to open my circle, over here, to truly let Robert in to my heart.

Opening my circle in general was another good move. My life had become so narrow and small. Yes, even in recovery. I was working from home, only leaving the house for dog walks, grocery runs and recovery meetings.

When I wasn't working, I was working. Or you could find me working. My therapist urged me to go on at least one social outing per week – and no, recovery meetings don't count. Wow. Even though I hated every outing as I was getting ready to embark on it, opening my circle of life was a brilliant way to enrich and enliven it.

While I knew I would never have another soul mate dog like Sawyer, I tried to focus on the joy he had brought to my life – rather than the pain of losing him. That kind of pain stays with you forever. It becomes a part of who you are.

It's up to us what we do with it. In my case, I wouldn't let it cripple me for the rest of my life. I would instead learn to live with it, to function while it sat there. It got less overbearing day by day.

As long as I promised to keep doing the social outings once a week, my therapist said I was ready to graduate.

"Did I get all A's?" I asked her.

"How do you feel?" she said.

"I'm rocking at least a B+."

Whee! I made it through the grief volcano. It had only taken about two years or so. And I even got additional souvenirs along the way.

★....LESSONS LEARNEd......⊙

All pets go to heaven (especially if they're named Sawyer).

The harder you grieve, the deeper you loved.

Grief is not something you get over. It's something you must move through. It changes you forever, making you stronger and more compassionate when you get out the other side.

Elmo and Gigi

There's a saying in recovery how you can "take what you want and leave the rest." Pick out what suggestions work for you, and leave the rest in the dust (or at least until a later date).

I've always been good at defying suggestions in general, but I've taken a lot of the tips I've heard in recovery. Yet I still know which suggestions in general to ignore, and one of those was not to get a new dog right away.

When Sawyer died, I was ready to get a new dog THAT NIGHT. But the shelter was already closed by the time the recovery meeting ended.

I was not trying to replace Sawyer. I knew that wasn't possible. But I also knew I needed something to fill that giant hole in the house. We still had Dini, but she was decidedly second fiddle. She couldn't step up to the first fiddle role. It wasn't in her DNA.

A new dog would not only fill the hole in the household, but it would give Dini a new friend. Most of all, it would serve as a huge distraction so I didn't have to deal with the grief as a giant tsunami.

A new dog would be like a little dam, let the grief trickle around the edges instead of swallowing me whole.

The new dog's name was Elmo. The minute I brought him home, he scampered to a back corner of the yard and wouldn't come near us for about three weeks.

Far cry from in-your-face Sawyer for sure. And it was Sawyer who told me to adopt Elmo in the first place.

Dini and I went to the shelter the day after Sawyer died. We wanted a biggish dog that Dini liked well enough not to bark at incessantly. I had already gone online and picked out several dogs from the available list.

First one had already been adopted. Second one, adopted. Third, fourth, fifth, also adopted.

What the heck?

Ended up that particular Saturday was free adoption day. No adoption fees at all. You just had to pay the $15 licensing fee. While that's good for a deal, that was not good for the selection. Only small yippy dogs were left. Or one big guy who wouldn't even look us in the eye.

Upon closer inspection, you could see the big guy had a mangled back foot. Giant scars down his sides. He was cowering in the back of the kennel, behind the little dog cot in there. People would peer in his cage, and he'd look at the floor.

"What's with this one?" I asked the shelter worker.

"Oh, he's been abused. It's so sad. We think maybe he was used as dog fighting bait."

They had found the dog tied to a tree with massive infections in his wounds and an equally massive respiratory infection. He was listed as a special needs dog, due to his injuries and background

While he had ignored every other person who had come near his cage, he actually looked up and moved a centimeter forward when he saw Dini.

We took him out to interact. He wouldn't come near me. Shrunk when I tried to touch him. But he took to Dini right away. Smelling her butt like they were old pals.

"That's the only dog he's shown any level of interest in," the shelter worker said.

Hmmm. That's a good sign. But the rest, I don't know.

We put him back in his kennel to walk through the shelter one more time.

As we were getting ready for another dog to come out and interact, I was standing right across from the cowering dog's kennel. He kept looking up quickly, then ducking his head when I'd catch him eyeing me. His eyes were big and brown and sad. So sad.

I don't know. Oh, I don't. Do we want to take that one home or not.

As I was mulling the situation in my head, Sawyer spoke to me.

"You gave me a chance. Give him one."

I told the shelter person to forget about the next dog interaction. We're going to take this cowering one home.

Yaay! Yippee! Yahoo! Word spread fast through the shelter workers. All burst into glee.

They were so happy someone was adopting cowering thing. He had been there for months and his time was nearly up. He had been a week or so away from euthanasia.

Although it took loads of time, persistence and a failed dog training class to finally get Elmo to trust us, it was worth it. Those sad eyes are now filled with gratitude.

One of Elmo's earliest gratitude moments came on his first trip to San Diego's dog beach. It was my first trip to that beach without Sawyer, and I had some of his ashes in tow to spread in the ocean he had loved so much.

I cried pretty much all the way there, and Dini and Elmo were good companions and distractions so I could stop crying long enough to keep a clear view of the road. It was a six-hour drive.

I also had a little knit blanket one of my friends had given me as a tribute to Sawyer. My plan was to head out to the beach at sunset to scatter the ashes and hurl the blanket into the sea where it would be swooshed away into eternity.

Rituals rock, and this was going to be a big solemn important one.

Night was nigh, so I headed out to the beach with the portion of Sawyer's ashes and the blanket. I got to the edge of the shore and spread his ashes OK. Well, the ashes spread OK but I wasn't feeling OK. My entire being was wracked with sobs and a new burst of anguish.

Then it came time to hurl the blanket into the sea, to be swooshed away for eternity. I hurled it and said a prayer, closed my eyes. *Goodbye, my Sawyer, my love.*

I few seconds later, something was brushing against my ankles. It was the blanket. The waves brought it right back to my feet.

I tried it again. Hurled the blanket into the sea, closed my eyes, said the prayer. There comes the blanket, bobbing and swirling right back to me.

Damn thing! I want to get this over with.

Once again. The same thing. Again, the same thing.

Apparently a man had been watching this. He came over to ask if I was alright since I was crying and, by now, cussing the blanket as I kept hurling it into the ocean.

I explained what I was doing in honor of my soul mate dog.

He had genuine compassion in his eyes. He also had a very relevant piece of knowledge to share.

"The tides are coming in right now," he said. "You can check when they're coming in or going out on a tide map. That blanket's going to keep coming back if you keep throwing it right now."

The next outgoing tide was at some weird hour in the middle of the night when I definitely didn't feel like hanging around the shoreline.

I made up a Plan B on the spot. Went and set the blanket gently at the foot of the main dog beach sign at the entrance. There it could remain forever, or at least until someone took it.

While I wasn't able to release the blanket into the great blue sea, I did get a mini-lesson on tides. As well as another message from Sawyer.

OK, Sawyer, fine, I get it. You aren't ever going to leave me. You're going to watch over me forever and ever, just like

Grandma P. And in between watching me, you'll be chasing demons out of heaven.

I quite like the idea, thank you.

Elmo's thank you came from the look in his eyes when I took him and Dini down to the beach shortly after our arrival. Dini made a barking beeline for the water, like she always did.

Elmo turned to look at me, incredulous. He looked at the ocean, looked back at me. Looked back at the ocean, looked back at me. It's as if he couldn't believe his eyes. No way is there water that big and open. And perfect for swimming!

I could see the stars and smiley faces swirling around his head as he bounded after Dini into the water. He swam and splashed and splished and swam. He was in his element, alive and vibrant. He had finally realized that life can be fun.

Elmo had become the most grateful hound I ever met. It warms my heart to see him so happy. So much so, Robert became a bit sick of hearing it.

"Yes, Ryn, you say that every other day."

I don't care. I'll keep saying it. I'll keep sharing and feeling the gratitude. And once in a while, I'll even cry those juicy plump tears of joy.

Even more joy came when Reggie entered into the mix. Originally named Ragnar, we renamed him Reggie but usually call him Gigi. He was a purebred Belgian Tervuren from a hippie farm in Vermont. They were the only breeders that had a Tervuren available when I needed one RIGHT NOW.

Again, he was not meant to replace Sawyer but to be another outlet for my dog love. Besides, Elmo was a short-haired down-to-earth dude and I needed another long-hair diva dog to pamper, brush and allow to shed all over the drapes, couch and carpet.

Reggie was flown from Vermont to Phoenix in a crate. When we let him out of the crate to get in the car, he immediately puked all over the place.

Ahhh, love at first sight.

He then snuggled up to me for the whole car ride home to Tucson. The breeders warned he was a lover and a jumper. He can't get enough love. And he can jump at least 6 feet into the air.

When we got home and I let Reggie run through the house and into the yard, Elmo immediately tried to eat him.

"No, Elmo. It's not a rabbit. It's your new brother."

All three dogs began to bond, with the two elders putting up with Reggie's ongoing antics. Like punching them in the face. Pulling the couch cushions out into the yard through the doggie door and then blaming it on Elmo. Or creating a swirl of chaos that just wouldn't stop, like a long-haired Tasmanian devil.

*.....Lessons Learned......

Life without dogs is like boots without socks. It's all wrong.

Dogs make great teachers. They live in the moment. They nap when they want to. They're never afraid to show their love.

Learning Curve

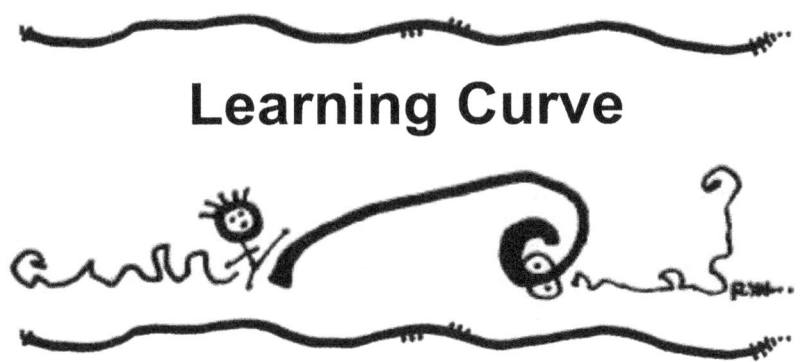

Dini died not too long after we got Reggie. The same thing that happened to Sawyer happened to her. The back half of her body stopped working. Vets once again had no clue. Dini could no longer walk or control her bladder.

She also got stand-offish and really cranky, like a nasty old Brooklyn landlord. Morty and I had one of those nasty old landlords in our first apartment. Her name was Petula and she spoke no English.

We lived on the second floor of the family's private house that had been divvied up into apartments.

When we'd come home from work or grocery shopping, Petula would be on the stoop with her cronies, a card table unfolded and blocking the front door. We'd smile, nod and point to the second floor.

She'd glare and begrudgingly move the table, muttering at us in Italian under her breath. Dini was acting like that. She was also doing the thing that dogs do – leaving the pack to go die in seclusion.

When we found Dini once again hiding in the edge of the yard beneath a bush, cranky and sad, we knew it was time to set her soul free. The ride to the vet was the happiest she had been in weeks, as if she somehow knew her suffering was going to be over.

All dogs go to heaven, and Dini went there, too. Instead of chasing demons out of heaven like Sawyer's doing, Dini is surely barking and barking and barking – even louder than the angels sing.

Because I had already been through the wringer when Sawyer died, I knew what to expect when Dini died. It still hurt. I still missed her. But I didn't have that soul mate bond with her, so it was a much smoother process.

I also didn't have the avalanche of old grief on the heels of the fresh grief. I had actually sat with, sat through and processed the feelings.

There's a saying in recovery that feelings aren't going to kill you – although it can certainly feel like it when you're working through something as powerful as grief you've been bottling up for decades.

Elmo was missing Dini, big time. Every time he'd see a fat black dog that looked kind of like her at the park or beach, he'd run up to her in happy expectation. Then it would turn around and alas, not Dini.

He kept that up for some time, until the message must have hit that Dini was home in heaven – which was where my Dad was also destined to visit soon.

Dad died in 2016, but his will to live had left about two years prior. Around the time of the Sawyer phone call when he said he wouldn't want to live if he were a dog that couldn't run and play.

Mom said Dad had been sitting down tying his shoes one day, struggling with the pain that had been eating him alive for about a decade. One of his arms would regularly go numb, become immobile. Even tying a shoe had become a massive burden.

She said he looked over at her and said flatly, "I'm done."

The fighting was over. He was ready to die. Even though he had declared this decision on a conscious level, his body kept him alive for another two years. Until it started breaking down, bit by bit, helped along by the pain. Helped along by the 15 or so different medications he was taking daily.

One to stop this, another to start that. A third to combat the effects of one and two. A fourth to combat the effects of the third and fifth. You get the idea.

Both my brother and I were in Michigan when it was obvious the time was coming. Hospice care had already been visiting the house. Mom was a frazzled mess, as she had the role of full-time care giver for years and years.

I had already made my amends to Dad, so my time with him was spent telling him how much I loved him. My brother went to talk to Dad, closed the bedroom door, and was in there for at least an hour.

Dad hung on a bit longer, until Mom gave him permission to die. That 3 a.m. we were all called into the bedroom. Dad died surrounded by Mom, brother, me and Chloe, the stray cat Mom had taken in a few years back.

That guttural scream came from my throat when I saw Dad on the stretcher as they were wheeling him out of the house.

Because he died at home in Michigan, the stomping grounds of Dr. Kevorkian, the police came to question us. Question Mom mainly. No, she didn't help her husband die in an assisted suicide.

The funeral parlor people left a rose on Dad's pillow.

I wrote an obituary to share on my blog. Mom, brother and I sat around in silence, reading all the condolences pouring into our respective Facebook pages as we broke the news to our connections.

My phone gave a loud alert, as if something important were coming in.

I looked – it was the Tucson internet bill.

What?! How DARE they! My dad had just died and they had the gall to send the monthly bill right when I was trying to grieve!

How could they think life just goes on as normal when my big, strong, wonderful beautiful man of a dad just died!

Yes, anger is one of the stages of grief. That anger morphed back into sorrow. But by the day of the funeral, I don't know how, it had transitioned into some kind of strength.

At one point during Dad's viewing services at the funeral home, everyone in the room was laughing so loud that one of the directors had to poke his head in to make sure we weren't all gone nuts.

Maybe we were, laughing uproariously at a funeral service. But then again, the Gargulinskis are delightfully unique.

It all started when it was time for my brother, Mom and I to share a few words about Dad. Sure, we stood up there at the microphone and sobbed like you see in TV movies.

But then we all shared snippets of our experiences with Dad that were downright hilarious. Fine, fond, fabulous memories that erupted laughter even when we all were crying.

Like one of Mom and Dad's early outings together, a wedding where she was dancing her heart out and Dad was sitting that one out at a table. She kicked up her leg and her shoe flew off – hitting Dad square in the forehead.

Or how my brother and Dad would toss the football out back with Joe Spruce, their name for the big tree that played wide receiver.

Or the time my Dad said he'd take my door off the hinges if I slammed it ONE MORE TIME. *Yeah right*, my surly teen-self had said. He's not going to go to all that trouble.

SLAM. I slammed it one more time. *So there!*

The next thing I knew, Dad was there with a screwdriver, taking the door off the frame.

A teen with no door on their room is a fate worth than death. Dad was always true to his word.

The stories swam, danced, and tickled laughter throughout the room. I looked over at Dad in his coffin, feeling bad he was missing all this. But then I realized he wasn't. He was in this room with us. He was laughing right along with us. He would always be in our hearts. He would always be my big beautiful Dad.

Sawyer and Dini's deaths had been a training ground of sorts, giving me the direction I needed to help Mom through Dad's death. I was honored I could help her. I was grateful to God for giving me the insights I could share.

Dad was cremated. They asked if we wanted his hardware, two knee replacement knee caps, two ball and socket joints from his two hip replacements. Of course, we wanted them. Or at least I did.

I made them into a tribute. Artwork. A metal spider wired together in honor of Dad. My doctor brother insisted I share the photo so he could send a copy to his knee and hip replacement pal. I believe the pal had been impressed.

✱.....Lessons Learned......☜

AA has a list of promises that eventually come true if you stay sober and embrace the steps. A big one came true for me during my dad's funeral: "We will intuitively know how to handle situations which used to baffle us."

But then again, all the promises are big ones. And they've all been coming true.

Since I mentioned the promises, I can't leave you without a rundown. Here they are, from the "Into Action" chapter of the Big Book:

We are going to know a new freedom and a new happiness.
We will not regret the past nor wish to shut the door on it.
We will comprehend the word serenity.
We will know peace.
No matter how far down the scale we have gone, we will see how our experience can benefit others.
The feeling of uselessness and self-pity will disappear.
We will lose interest in selfish things and gain interest in our fellows.
Self-seeking will slip away.
Our whole attitude and outlook upon life will change.

Fear of people and economic insecurity will leave us.
We will intuitively know how to handle situations which used to baffle us.
We will suddenly realize that God is doing for us what we could not do for ourselves.

Jumping the Shark

With all that death going on, you might think all I did in Tucson was sit around and grieve. While I certainly did a lot of grieving there, I did even more growing.

And the three deaths didn't happen in quick succession. They were spaced at least a year or so apart. It just made sense to put them all together to support the notion that things happen in threes. Whew. Those were three big ones.

The next set of threes were all about discovery. By now I had about 19 years in recovery, a solid freelance writing and art career, two dogs that were young enough to hopefully stick around for several more years (knock wood), and a loving, long-term relationship.

I was also bored out of my freakin' mind.

Yes, being a self-employed artist and writer had long been my dream job. But my dream job had now become my job-job.

Day in, day out, the same old same old same old. Not only that, but I had been stuck at the same income level for about 10 years. No matter how many higher-paying clients I snagged or barn-sized cat signs I sold, my income level stayed stagnant.

It was definitely time to make a change.

I read a bunch of books on psychic powers, thinking I could just segue into a career helping to solve crimes and connecting people on earth with their loved ones in heaven.

I'd be better than the psychic I once went to in Brooklyn in the middle of the night. Morty and I had had a fight, so I ran out of the house in an impulsive huff. So impulsively, I was halfway down the block before I realized I was barefoot.

The street was dark. Everything was closed. Except for one sign that was still lit. Psychic Rose, located on the second floor of a building on Bensonhurst's 86th Street.

I stumbled into her parlor, half-drunk, barefoot, and shaking with rage.

"You are very angry," she told me. "And confused."

Wow. This woman was spot-on.

If she got me to hand over $10 just for that, I could make even more money with readings that were actually meaningful.

Since I never really moved forward with it, it didn't work. And since I never bothered to go through the palm reading book, that idea didn't pan out, either.

Tarot cards – I got this one!

I studied, meditated on the cards, bought a variety of decks, and was improving my intuitive readings by doing them for free.

People both enjoyed and learned a lot from them. But I had yet to get a paying tarot customer.

Next.

I know. Homicide detective!

While that idea may seem to have come out of far left field, it really didn't. It came out of close left field. I always had three dream jobs topping my list. Writer and artist was number one, followed by homicide detective and mortician.

Although I had long been fascinated by road kill and other dead things when I was a shade younger, the allure had worn off a bit when I figured out why. I was scared to death of death – or rather, the idea of becoming nothing after you died.

But by now I had read enough, learned enough and strengthened my faith enough to know in my heart there is an afterlife. And it's a good one. Not only does your soul live forever – but you get to be YOU. In short, even if I come back as a goat or gadfly, it will be a goat or gadfly named Ryn.

Skulls, skeletons and creepy things were still close to my heart, but I no longer felt the urge to photograph every chunk of road kill on the shoulder of the road. And I didn't think being around dead people and the stench of the formaldehyde all day would be all that conducive to my mental health.

That left homicide detective. I had just missed the Tucson Police Department's annual exam, but I had time to move forward with the Pima County Sheriff's Department. I downloaded an outline of everything I had to pass for both the written and physical exam.

I knew I'd have to start at the start and work years before I could advance to homicide detective. This was a mondo drawback. But I was bored enough with my current rut to give it a go.

I glanced down the list of tasks that would be part of the physical exam.

Drag 150 pounds of dead weight. Check. Run however long in whatever amount of time. Check. Jump over a 6-foot wall.

What?! They only hire Superman offspring?

Although I had run hurdles in middle school, none of them were 6 feet tall. Oh, it appears you could jump over the wall after you scaled up it, not just jump over in one fell swoop.

It was still a challenge. But it was also my luck that our Tucson subdivision was surrounded by 6-foot stone walls that would make for perfect practicing.

The walls in our own backyard were lower than 6 feet, and they were overrun with plant life and artwork. So I found a nice community wall at the front of the neighborhood that had enough room to run, scale, get over, land.

Every day before the weather turned scorching, I'd be out at the front of the subdivision so I could run, scale, get over and land. Two things about this whole endeavor amazed me.

The first was that I actually COULD run, scale, get over and land on the other side of a 6-foot wall. Wohooo!

It's not like I was a couch potato – I exercised every day – but I had also read about the dreaded "Sitting Disease." Headlines screamed that it was "the new smoking." You might as well start digging your grave now if you sit around for the majority of the day.

Writing work is all sitting. Well, mostly sitting. My treadmill has a little shelf for my computer. Being a Gemini also means I have the burning urge to get up from my chair about five times an hour to do this, do that, or the other thing.

The second that amazed me about the neighborhood wall scaling was that no one called the cops or somehow wrote up some kind of community violation over my weeks of practicing.

Heck, this was one of the anal homeowner association places that once mailed us a violation for having the handle of a tall rake sticking up and visible over the top of our back wall.

If we had 6-foot walls around our backyard, mind you, that wouldn't have been a problem.

The physical exam was on my schedule, but the written exam came first. It started with a big welcome speech that said this was the start of a 20-year career. And the starting pay was less than I was currently making as a self-employed writer and artist.

Add leaving the house to actually drive through the horror of Tucson traffic every day, and this job was losing its appeal. Especially the 20-year thing. I was 49, or about the age most sheriff deputies or detectives are eligible to retire – not start.

I took the written exam anyway. Got an 87. The toughest section had you look at an image for one minute and then answer a ton of questions about what you saw.

"How many one-way streets were there?"
"Which direction was the red car heading on the street?"
"Was there a red car or was it a truck?"
"How many people were on the sidewalk?"
"What did the sign on the easternmost building say?"

Natural curiosity and a background as a reporter gave me an edge on that stuff. It was all about being aware of your surroundings. But it was still tough. I'd love to see how those people who hog the supermarket aisles would do on the observation section.

You know the folks, with their overflowing carts and fat butts blocking the entire aisle so even Twiggy couldn't get through. They apparently have no clue of anything or anyone around them.

I cancelled the sheriff department's physical exam and did a random internet search for what I should do next. I put in keywords related to what I knew, what I enjoyed, what I wanted to do.

"Get certified in recovery coaching," came up.

Hey, I found my next calling.

I entered a dual program for certification in professional life coaching and professional recovery coaching. Whoa, did I learn a ton. I already had a strong foundation in recovery from my own experience, but the program opened my eyes to deeper insights and intriguing information.

Like that thing called "reptile brain." It's a phenomenon associated with addiction where the brain is actually reduced to the level of a reptile. The only concerns are eating, sleeping, copulating and getting the next fix. Reptiles will attack anything or anyone that gets in the way of those needs.

The life coaching modules were just as intriguing. It took me about a year or so to get through it all. I was officially certified. Let the coaching clients roll in!

They didn't.

I got a few clients here and there, but nothing steady. Even AFTER joining a hardcore networking group that brought zillions of leads to other professions. Sigh. It seemed the harder I pushed at getting coaching clients, the more writing assignments came my way.

Bigger and better writing assignments. And my pay actually started to increase.

An increase in pay only happened after going deep and working on my relationship with money. The "Financial Alchemy" workbook played a major role, as did seeing a wealth coach with an hourly rate that cost nearly as much as my mortgage payment.

I once heard you can't charge coaching fees that are higher than you'd be willing to pay. I figured paying ridiculous amounts paved the way for charging ridiculous amounts. Or at least that's what I told myself. In reality, I was desperate for a breakthrough out of my rut.

As scaling the 6-foot wall would attest, I was willing to try just about anything.

A big breakthrough did come from one major insight and one reading suggestion from the high-priced wealth coach. The major insight was that, despite all my work to love myself and bolster my self-esteem, a part of me still felt unworthy.

The Universe is not going to send higher pay to someone who feels that don't deserve it.

The coach also told me to read the book "The Big Leap." Holy moly. It's all about the four major ways we sabotage our own success. So not only did I feel I wasn't deserving of more pay, but I was subconsciously sabotaging any success at getting it.

This was golden. This was great!

So how do I change it?

Finding the source of the feelings of unworthiness was a major turning point.

While I couldn't pinpoint a single episode, I could unearth several incidents from early childhood: being made fun of for my last name; the dark birthmark on my left cheek (which faded once I reached adulthood); the missing front tooth I had knocked out during a fall when I was 2 years old.

I also recall bursting into a room full of adults to show off my very first illustrated story, proclaiming, "I want to be an artist and writer!"

"That's nice dear," said one of them, "But what will you do for money?"

Once such ideas are planted in our heads, we then spend the rest of our lives looking for evidence to support them. Being belittled, called weird, and told I was not good enough to make it as a writer and artist had over the years had become the ultimate truth ingrained in my subconscious.

It was time to dismiss the previous stories as lies, form new beliefs, and rewrite the story. I could then move forward collecting evidence to reprogram my subconscious.

I AM worthy. I AM good enough to make loads of money as an artist and writer. I DESERVE the money. I DESERVE happiness. I DESERVE all the goodness in the world!

And yes, I'm still weird – and dang proud of it!

★.....LESSONS LEARNED......℮

If you're feeling blocked, go deep. Be fearless. You may be amazed at the unknown blockages you find.

Whenever you're not sure what to do next, try a bunch of different things to see which feels best. Or you can always flip a coin.

Better than Caffeine

If you think reprogramming the subconscious on an emotional and intellectual level is fun, just wait until you see what happens when you start adding energy work into the mix.

We're all made up of energy. Everything is made up of energy. Energy work focuses on bringing high-vibrational healing energy into our body, minds and souls.

My energy work journey started with Reiki. And only because my elbows hurt.

There must be something to that sitting disease, especially when you work on a computer for years with no ergonomic setup. I ended up with double tendonitis, with both elbows constantly throbbing in excruciating pain.

Pain killers were out. They're too addictive. They also only treat the symptoms, not the root cause of the problem. Getting a new chair, new mouse pad and adjusting the height of my computer and keyboard would help going forward.

But nothing was helping to get rid of the current agony. Copper-infused elbow sleeves. Essential oils. Nothing.

Until I discovered Reiki. I ran across Reiki while looking for a way to get rid of the pain. And instead of booking a session to see what it was all about, I instead decided to go for the gold.

Let's get certified as a Reiki practitioner!

So I did.

I really had no idea what Reiki even was. In fact, in my head I had mixed it up with reflexology. Reiki is the channeling of divine healing energy from the heavens, through the practitioner, into you.

It's kind of like acupuncture but without the needles. The healing energy is meant to unblock and enhance your flow of life force energy on the physical, mental, emotional and spiritual levels.

Reflexology is a healing method that focuses on different areas of your feet, which correspond to different areas throughout your body. Oops. At least they both start with the letter R.

The Reiki certification process involved a five-hour class with a Tucson Reiki Master. Six of us met at her house, read a manual all about Reiki, learned the hand positions practitioners use during the sessions, and did some hands-on training.

It also involved an attunement. This is a Reiki initiation process where you sit in a chair while the practitioner walks around you to "seal" the Reiki symbols into your being for all eternity.

Coooooooool.

The experience was great, but I didn't know just HOW great it was until I got home and tried to go about my regular routine. Oh. My. God. My being was so infused with Reiki, I was bouncing off the walls.

I was floating. I was flying. I was laughing. Forget about trying to do work, because nothing at all on this earthly plane mattered. All that mattered was the divine healing energy.

Woohoo! Yippee! Yeehaw!

I even created a sticker: "Reiki: Better than Caffeine."

I spent the next three or four days on a cloud that swirled faster than a blender and soared higher than the sun. The Reiki energy eventually settled in, allowing me to get some work done by the middle of the following week.

There are three levels of Reiki certification. And I needed the next two, pronto.

Reiki master lady recommended we wait a few months between attunements. For obvious reasons. I still had to be able to work, after all. That powerful surge of energy needed more time than a week to settle.

Reiki Level I certification gives you the basics to be a Reiki practitioner to give Reiki to yourself and others.

Level II certification gives you the first set of Reiki symbols, enabling you to send Reiki across time, space and geographical distances.

Level III Master/Teacher certification gives you the second set of Reiki symbols, which lets you initiate others into Reiki.

I was going all the way, baby – and I wasn't looking back.

My joy of Reiki prompted me to look into other types of energy work.

What else is out there? What more can I learn? Tell me, Universe, what's next?

Another seemingly random internet search landed me on a certification program for integrative hypnosis.

Yes. Fabulous. Amazing! Let's do it.

What the hell is it?

The certification was for a five-year program that covered DNA activation, crystal therapy, all levels of Reiki, hypnosis for healing, hypnobirthing, and a few other incredible things that made my heart flutter with glee.

I was SOOOOOOO in!

Or at least I was until I looked at the price tag: $10,000.

When I clicked on the financial assistance tab, I saw the organization offered scholarships. Let's apply and see what happens. The application involved a ton of questions and several essays, one of which that asked where you see yourself at the end of the program.

"I see myself on an amphitheater stage, cracking jokes and helping people make magic in their lives!"

I got in.

Three years later, I was still officially in the first year of study. The premise of the program is great, but it's also a new organization with growing pains. More like growing agony.

The study plan, reading list, meditation schedule and online classes have been rearranged, unavailable, haphazardly available and rearranged again.

I got frustrated enough to nearly withdraw twice. But I get drawn back in by the promise of what's yet to come.

Although it's been a tough and stressful road, I have to say I have learned a lot and changed considerably. I feel lighter, brighter and happier. I also have the lowdown on all that so-called "junk DNA" that we never use is not junk at all.

One belief is that the untapped DNA in our makeup is where all the secrets to spiritual connections reside. That's what the DNA attunements were all about. Waking that stuff up.

Sacred geometry, beings of lights, ascended masters, Mother Earth, multi-dimensional healing, fifth-dimensional living, activations, the great central sun, the source of all that is.

All of it expands your mind beyond the dismal third dimension, which is the outer world on earth where things are largely driven by materialism and fear.

If we instead go inward and upward we can experience higher dimensions of reality. Head up into the fourth and fifth dimensions, and we get peace, joy, happiness and unconditional love.

No wonder I had been such a huge fan of LSD and other psychedelics.

Heck, one time I ate a whole bag of magic mushrooms and wasn't even fazed. It was back in the Jax and Big John days when Jerry Garcia was still alive and the Grateful Dead was playing at Madison Square Garden.

I didn't give a squat about the concert. But I wanted to check out the notorious Dead Head scene and score some drugs.

No one had LSD, but I did get a baggie of magic mushrooms. I told the guy who sold it to me he couldn't leave my side until they started working, recalling how I got ripped off my first day in New York City. This wasn't going to happen again.

I ate one or two of the mushrooms and waited. Nothing. So I ate the whole bag. The guy's eyes popped out of his head when he saw what I was doing. About two seconds later, I told him he could go now. They were working just fine.

Then I tried to take the subway home.

Not a good move.

Thankfully, a car full of four New Jerseyites leaving the concert happened to stop and offer a ride back to Jax's place on Avenue A. Perhaps my twirling and screaming near the intersection by the subway entranced gave them a clue that I could use some help.

I had them laughing the whole way back. I then saw crickets dancing on the apartment walls, keeping time to Jimi Hendrix's "Up from the Skies."

That Hendrix song is still one of my favorite tunes. Exploring alternate dimensions must be in my blood. And energy work gave me a way to do it that didn't involve subways, magic mushrooms, or screaming wildly in the streets for someone from New Jersey to drive me home.

My whole life I've been searching for that place of joy, happiness and unconditional love. It's been right here inside me all along.

It's inside all of us. If we quiet down long enough to listen, to connect with that spiritual place nestled deep in our souls, we can tap into it.

We are then blessed with all the support, resources, encouragement, strength and love we need, more than enough to share with everyone around us – and even the entire world.

It's magic, I'm telling ya. Pure magic.

★·····LESSONS LEARNEd·····℮

The only thing better than tapping into the magic is being able to share the magic with others.

Water World

Even with the Reiki, DNA attunements, fifth-dimensional living and my income increase, there was still another yearning in my soul. That yearning was to once again live near water.

I had grown up in the Great Lake State of Michigan. Mom even has a photo of me, a fully-clothed 3-year-old in the middle of winter, grinning ear to ear after making a beeline into the frigid waters of Lake Huron.

I then ran away to New York City, where I walked the Brooklyn Bridge monthly and visited Coney Island weekly (at least in the summer). Water, water, everywhere. And no, I wouldn't drink it. Especially if it came from the East River.

New Mexico gave me a water shortage, although I did get a little blue plastic pool for the backyard. The Pacific Northwest brought me back to the ocean, but its glory was offset by way too much rain.

The Tucson desert was downright incredible. It's a magical place that baked the dampness out of my soul and gave me a surreal plateau to blossom and grow.

But, dammit, I needed my water back. Where could we go to live near the water?

By now the world was getting stupid, and California's laws were leading the stupidity race. It was also way too expensive.

After leaving New York, I saw how much more house and land you could get for a fraction of the cost just about anywhere else. Anywhere else except California. Cross it off the list.

Water or not, anything north of Tucson would be too cold. Cross off Washington, Oregon, and most of the Eastern Seaboard. Texas had the Gulf of Mexico, but it still got cold. Needed something with a southern tip. That left one state that fit the bill.

"Hey Robert, what do you think about moving to Florida?"

"Doing what?!"

"Good. You didn't say no. Consider it done."

There's a quote that notes: "When the student is ready, the teacher appears."

It seemed to have adjusted itself for our circumstances. "When the water-lover is ready, the Florida house appears."

Once the idea of moving to Florida was planted firmly in my soul, a new Florida house manifested within 10 days.

It was like I wished it to be, and it happened. Evidently, I was energetically aligned to receive what I asked for. I knew we deserved it. And I was truly ready to let go of the old to embrace the new.

Tucson had the distinct flavor of being done. And it was the first time I was moving in a bid to move toward something I wanted – instead of run away from something I didn't.

It was incredible. I went from thinking we were stuck in Tucson because of that balloon payment on the mortgage to actually moving forward with a brand-new house in Florida. All in less than two weeks.

That didn't mean we could move in two weeks. We had to wait until the new house was built, which would be about six months down the road.

We also had to secure the new mortgage, get the Tucson house ready for sale, and thank my mom to heaven and back for supplementing our down payment so we could buy a brand-new house made of cinderblocks instead of a crummy old one made of spongy wood.

Oh yeah. We also had to pack. Pack. And pack. And then pack some more. Once we started the packing train, it immediately went off the rails.

As the creative type who thinks pretty much every piece of debris either looks useful or could be used in an art project, there was so much junk to pack.

Just when we thought we made a dent, we'd turn around to see 800 more things that still needed boxes. And I donated a lot. A hell of a lot. Truck loads worth of a lot. I also listed oodles of stuff on an online marketplace AND had a huge yard sale.

I think all of Robert's things fit in a dozen boxes. I won't even give you the count of how many boxes my jumbles of junk required. And most of it WAS junk. Things I didn't even remember I had. Like three different batons. Or all those medieval weapons from yard sales over the years.

"Hey Robert, remember when I wanted to re-learn how to twirl a baton? Did you know I have an actual medieval mace thing?"

You tend to accumulate a lot of stuff when you spend 14 years in the same house, especially when the garage and yard give you extra room to stash stuff. Thank God Tucson doesn't have basements.

We were so stressed and excited about moving to Florida, neither one of us could sleep the day before we supposed to leave. So we said to hell with it and hopped in our vehicles for Florida at 3 a.m. – only to spend the next two hours getting lost as we were trying to get out of Tucson.

Guess it wasn't much of a time saver. A time saver was desperately needed, as we were racing against the clock. We had to get to Florida to sign the closing documents by Thursday, December 31. All offices were closed for New Year's Day on Friday, and the weekend hit right after that.

We'd have to spend three extra days in a hotel if we didn't make it. We'd also have a big chunk of extra taxes to pay for not submitting certain paperwork by the end of the previous year. We couldn't submit that paperwork until we closed on the house. We couldn't close on the house until we got there.

We couldn't get there unless we finally got the bleep out of Tucson!

Wow, we had our our first walkie-talkie fight!

We invested in walkie-talkies. Robert drove his truck, packed to the hilt inside and outside. I drove my car, packed with the two big dogs.

One more thing. We needed to be on schedule for the movers. They said it would be on its way to Florida from Tucson the minute they picked it up.

If we weren't yet in the house when the movers got there, the stuff would have to go into storage to the tune of hundreds of dollars a day. The moving contract was a real piece of work. Enough fine print to make your head spin.

We finally got out of Tucson, then out of Arizona, and made a quick blip through New Mexico. We then entered Texas for what seemed like six weeks.

The whole trip was about 2,100 miles, and Texas easily ate up at least 700 of those miles. The scenery and smellery were all the same. Open fields. Brown brush. Wave of cow manure aroma. Open fields. Brown brush. Wave of cow manure aroma.

At least the wave of cow manure aroma jostled you awake when highway hypnosis hit. And at least we didn't nearly crash and burn like we did in Louisiana.

Although we were in different vehicles, we both fell prey to the Louisiana highway deathtrap. You're zooming along on the highway, when all of a sudden – the road runs out.

No warning signs. No arrows on the pavement. No nothing. The inner left lane on the highway. Just. Stops. The book cover from Shel Silverstein's "Where the Sidewalk Ends" came immediately to mind – right after the image of my coffin, of course.

Mississippi, Alabama and Georgia were again quick blips. Don't remember much except the dogs are still horrible about getting out at rest stops to pee.

They'll bound out of the car like they're on fire, run around in a circle without peeing, and then run back to the car door as if they're being chased by giant dog-eating wombats.

Pensacola, Florida, sticks out in my head because it had the worst motel yet. We had booked all our motel rooms blindly, just making sure it was a place not too far from the highway exit that allowed dogs. You can imagine what we ended up with.

Drug dens, every one of them. I knew the places all too well. I had lived in them. They were the same type of seedy places where Big John and I lived at throughout New York City. One big switch was that I no longer felt comfortable in such an environment.

Yahoo! for recovery.

But that didn't mean yahoo! for our pickup bed full of worldly possessions. It would have taken at least an hour to unpack the mass and bring it all in the motel room, so we left all kinds of whatever strapped in the back of Robert's truck.

When we weren't tossing and turning in a bed where someone was probably murdered, we were taking turns looking out the window into the parking lot.

"Stuff is still there."

"Stuff is still there."

"Stuff is still there."

"No one's stolen it yet."

"Don't say it like that!" I admonished Robert. "You know that just calls it to us."

You need to be careful with your words. The Universe listens to every single thing you say, and then it happily tries to deliver. The only problem is, it doesn't understand nuances. And it doesn't understand negatives, like when you say "Don't trip."

How many times have you said that to someone only to have them trip the next instant? A bunch. That's because all the Universe hears is "trip," and it delivers the stumble.

If you put the words "stole" and "stuff" together, you're just asking for thievery.

Hey! I bet that's what happened with the road ending abruptly in Louisiana!

One of us must have inadvertently said something like, "I wish this stupid highway would end already."

And then it did.

....LESSONS LEARNED.....

Anyone who says "It's all about the journey, not the destination," has never been on a three-day road trip from Tucson, Arizona, to Cape Coral, Florida, with two big dogs in tow.

Florida – Dec. 31, 2020

We made it! Made it to the title company before they closed on New Year's Eve, signed the papers, waited for whatever last thing made us sit there for an hour on pins and needles, and then finally got the key.

Our new Florida house! Our new Florida house!

The builder and our wonderful Florida Realtor came with us to give us the lowdown on things we needed to know – like where the hurricane shutters were stored in the garage and how to put them up if we ever needed to.

I was confident we wouldn't. After all, I picked Cape Coral, Florida, because it was near Fort Myers. Thomas Edison built his winter estate in Fort Myers because, after much calculation, he determined this area on the Gulf Coast was the least likely to be hit by hurricanes.

Hurricanes were the last thing on our minds. We were too busy oohing and ahhing over the shiny white tile kitchen and crisp white cabinets. I think Florida has an unwritten rule that at least 97% of a home's interior has to be white.

All was beautiful, gorgeous, brand new! It was the first time either Robert or I lived in a brand-new house. It was also a house we were truly sharing. When he moved in to my Tucson house, it was already filled up with junk.

This way we could fill it up with junk as a joint effort. But right now it was so fresh and clean and new, I felt like I should be wearing gloves and booties just walking through it.

Reggie took care of that vibe right quick. When we let the dogs in, he made a beeline for the master bedroom, squatted in the middle of the grey-white carpet, and took a big doggie dump.

The beach. The beach. The beach!

One of my driving forces for moving to Florida was to go to the beach as frequently as possible. A little beach in Cape Coral made that possible.

I happily eased into the best Saturday routine. I found a morning AA meeting in a gazebo at a park by the river. Then I'd drive 10 minutes to the little family beach by the river.

It was a small beach that was never overly crowded. It had a distinct family and locals vibe without the mounds of screaming tourists.

Tourists typically hit the bigger beaches on the Gulf of Mexico or the Atlantic Ocean.

This was a darling little beach along the Caloosahatchee River with its fair share of palm trees, a few pavilions and a retirement center across the street that looked like it was built in 1963. Perfect.

If you got bored with perfect, you did get a bit of strangeness or drama from time to time. The strangeness came every time mankini man showed up. To each his own, sure, but this guy would show up to the small family beach in a skimpy red mankini.

Yeah, it was kind of creepy. And much like a car wreck. You couldn't help but stare at him traipsing back and forth along the sand, wondering why the hell he'd wear this kind of outfit to a little family beach.

The bit of drama came from an actual shark attack in the brackish river waters. I've been a huge fan of sharks ever since I saw "Jaws" at a drive-in at the age of 6.

My parents had taken me along, perhaps figuring a 6-year-old wouldn't absorb much of the movie when she was busy throwing her Raggedy Ann doll out the rolled-down car window.

I remember coming home from the movie and my dad telling me to be careful when I opened my bedroom door.

"Water is going to come whooshing out with a shark in it!"

Dad had a way with young children. I've feared and revered sharks ever since.

I also fell in love with the whole "Jaws" story. Must have read the novel at least six times, seen the movie a dozen or more. Wore out both my "Jaws" videocassette and DVD. That's dedication.

While I've seen plenty of sharks through glass in aquariums, I never saw a real one in real life. Until one sunny day at the Caloosahatchee River.

I was taking a quick dip in the water. My rule for any body of water that may contain sharks is to go up to my waist and then sit down.

This way the water still goes up to my neck, giving me the full-body-immersion-in-water experience, but with significantly less of a risk of being ripped in half by a Great White.

So I was taking that dip, and I noticed a swarm of seagulls circling around like fast-motion maniacs overhead. I watched them kind of dive bomb a couple of swimmers directly behind me.

I didn't know why they would act like that, but I had a feeling I might want to get out of the water.

I walked the 10 or steps to shore, with the two swimmers directly behind me.

"Is that usual?" one swimmer lady asked me.

"Is what usual?"

"Shark attacks at this beach," she said, pointing to a thrashing mass of blood red water down the shore a bit, maybe 15 feet from the shoreline.

Whoa. The thrashing mass was a shark attacking something (not a human). The telltale fin would pop up above the waterline, disappear, pop back up. Yep. Just like in the movies! That was a shark all right. All the seagulls were swarming to get bits and pieces of the shredded-up detritus.

Double whoa. A real-life shark attack! Right here at my favorite beach! How thrilling can you get?!

Just like everything in Arizona is armed, it seems most things in Florida can easily kill you. Sharks. Alligators. Poisonous snakes. Looking too long at a mankini.

Inauguration

The rule is that you don't get to be an official Floridian until you've lived through a hurricane. While I was more than fine and dandy to live without that designation, apparently Hurricane Ian was not.

He came roaring through our world on Sept. 28, 2022. What a pain.

Not only did we get inaugurated into Florida-dom with a hurricane that had been expected to miss us until it made a sudden unexpected turn to head right through our backyard, but it had to be a Category 4 hurricane with winds at 149.9 mph.

Category 5 is the highest you can go.

"It must be terrifying!" people say when you tell them you were in the path of a hurricane. And it is – for about the first five minutes. Then it just turns maddening.

Actually, the experience is maddening even before the hurricane hits. Since Ian was brewing up to be a torrential storm, and the media absolutely loves scaring people, panicky headlines penetrated the area for about a week prior to the hurricane's arrival.

People were hoarding water, batteries and potato chips. Gas station lines snaked out into the streets. Neighbors started putting up their hurricane shutters. While I tried to talk Robert out of it for as long as possible, we finally followed suit.

Metal plates bolted over all the windows made the house dark and creepy, like we were living in a cave. Sure, that would have been a wonderful feel during my drinking days, but I have since come to love the light.

I knew the shutters would make me cranky. They did. At least I talked him out of leaving the shutters off the back sliding glass door so we could still go out into the backyard.

I was out on the lanai the day the hurricane was supposed to hit land, wondering when we should finally put the shutters on the back sliding glass door.

The wind suddenly turned from its ongoing low-motor hum into a screeching banshee – as something brown and clunky zipped past the lanai like a missile.

I guess now would be a good time to put up the last of the shutters.

But by that time, it was already too late. Trying to do anything outside in the suddenly ferocious winds would be about as smart as doing a backflip on the tip of the Eiffel Tower.

The brown flying thing started off my five minutes of terror. The howling wind that ensued continuously fueled the ongoing madness.

More madness came when the power and internet went out soon after the howling winds hit. It was right after Robert said, "I'm surprised the power is still on."

We had a generator, so we had figured we'd be good. But we forgot someone had to go outside to turn it on. *Oops*. Not out in this. It would have to wait.

Wait until the fence blew away. Wait until the yard was destroyed. Wait until the dogs' bladders were about to burst because they couldn't go outside to do their business.

Wait until trees were ripped out from their roots. Neighboring roofs were blown to smithereens. And the siding was stripped off the two-story house across the street.

Then, and only then, after 18 hours of sheer madness, did the wind finally stop.

The first thing I did was take the dogs out. The second was scour the neighborhood for our scattered fiberglass fence pieces. The third was stare and stare and stare some more at what used to be a neat and nifty neighborhood.

It now looked like a war zone.

Stop signs were turned sideways. A car windshield was shattered. Tree parts littered the streets and lawns. A big blue thing that looked like a mattress was propped in a nearby cluster of weeds, leaves and bushes.

Thankfully we had waited for a cement-block house to be built instead of buying the spongy-wood house I wanted just because it was available immediately. Our house had a missing gutter and dent in the soffit. The big bad wolf of a hurricane may have wreaked havoc on many other houses, but ours withstood the storm like a champ.

It took a full five days to clear all the debris out our yard, and then another three months before any fence company could come to fix our fence. We propped up the fence pieces we had into a makeshift barrier so the dogs wouldn't go roaming out into the wilds.

Even though Elmo and Gigi typically refuse to venture farther than the end of the driveway when I take them on their walks, they'd gleefully take advantage of an opening in the fence. I know because I tested it. Found Elmo barking his head off some five houses down the road.

The whole area was a jumbled mess. No electricity or internet throughout the entire city. That meant no stop lights, no stores open, no gas stations to replenish the gas for our generator. We had to use it sparingly.

Of course, it was late September and easily in the 90-degree zone every day. You think the biggest thing you'd miss is the air conditioner – until you realize your well pump needs electricity to run and you really, really need a shower.

We had no electricity for about 12 days. No internet for 25 days. Since all my writing, workshops, art shipping labels and other money-making functions required the internet, I couldn't work for pretty much the entire month of October.

And I thought I was cranky when the hurricane shutters went up. The crankiness mixed with fear when we didn't have electricity or the internet for an extended period.

We're going to die without electricity! We'll end up eating peanut butter and stale rice cakes for the rest of our lives! What happens when we run out of food and water?! We'll smell like B.O. forever and ever!

And without the internet, whew, a double whammy.

I'll go broke! My clients will leave me! I'll no longer have any writing work or Reiki workshops to go back to!

As backwards as it seems, the fear that came with living without the internet was scarier than living through the howling winds. I can't work from home and make money without the internet. It is pretty scary that we're so dependent on electric and digital everything.

But even scarier was the stupid guilt I was feeling, like it was somehow my fault.

Yes, I hatched this masterplan so I wouldn't have to work for a month. Teehee.

Come to think of it, I actually did scream to the Universe that I was burnt out and needed time off.

Be careful what you wish for. You just might get a hurricane.

Months after the storm hit, the city of Cape Coral was still rebuilding itself. The entire area was still recovering. In at least one supermarket, prices had been jacked to the moon "to make up for the hurricane."

There was even a boat on a median on the way to my beloved beach – which was slated to remain closed "for the foreseeable future."

Here's where I had a choice. I could focus on the devastation of the hurricane, bemoan my beloved beach closing, and curse Thomas Edison to hell and back for putting too much faith in his predictions that hurricanes are least likely to hit the area where I live.

This kind of thinking would inevitably make me cranky. I'm absolutely no fun when I'm cranky. Even my dogs leave the room when the crankiness comes in.

My other choice was to look at the positive. Our family was still alive, including most of the plants and trees in our yard. Our house withstood Hurricane Ian, the fifth most powerful storm to ever hit the U.S.

The park and my recovery meetings were still there. Ian didn't even make a dent in the wooden gazebo we meet under every Saturday morning.

Living through a hurricane made us official Floridians. Mom helped me with funds to make up for my lack of income without the internet. And when the internet was finally restored, my clients and part-time job were still waiting for me.

At least until the New Year came.

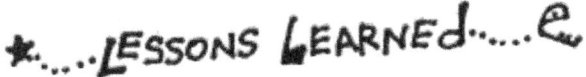

With enough persistence and practice, you can start to see the positive side of just about anything.

Happy New Year! You're Fired

Yeah, that's pretty much what happened to me when I logged in to work on Jan. 3 for the part-time gig I've held for the past two years.

The boss asked if I had a minute for a Zoom call. I told him sure, thinking he wanted to talk about the next project. He didn't.

"We did our 2023 budget," he said, "and your position isn't in it. Effective at the end of today."

Happy New Year to you, too, right?

The funny thing is, I had just created my first EVER crystal grid – to manifest abundance – the night before.

Some abundance.

Then it hit me.

This was a blessing to make way for the bigger, better and more glorious things to come. It was opening the door to the abundance that could not be had with this gig clogging up my schedule.

How can you invite in the new and beautiful if the old and stale is still hanging around?

The job had run its course (ask Robert, who had to listen to the moaning). The two 10-hour days had been wearing me thin, but I was too afraid to let it go on my own. It was once again God's way of doing for me what I could not do for myself.

I am excited to see what bigger and better things are in store. And I got a glimpse of a few already with a packed schedule for the next week and a half.

It also gave me the additional time I needed to finish this book...and get even more abundance flowing.

In fact, I wasn't fired at all. I was set free. Set free to do my thing without a weekly albatross. Set free to sleep past 4 a.m. on Mondays and Tuesdays. Set free to nap every. Single. Day.

Working through my usual naptime was one of my biggest beefs about the gig. That, and the tracking software that recorded my every single move on the computer to make sure I was working instead of looking up my horoscope or buying more crystals to add to my collection.

Here again I was faced with a choice. How am I going to deal with this situation? Look at the positive, or fester in the negative?

Of course, a major whoosh of feelings came up right after I was hit with the totally unexpected news of being fired. Once the shock wore off, I got to sit through a flurry of fun feelings. Fear cried about losing a chunk of steady income.

Betrayal and anger sneered about sticking with the company through three different content managers over a two-year period.

This is how you thank me?!

Unworthiness tried to weasel its way in, telling me they let me go because I am a terrible awful person and even worse employee – even though the man who fired me told me three times it wasn't.

I didn't let the unworthiness in. I have done way too much work around the topic to get tricked into believing it. I also have way too much evidence that states otherwise.

Grief even poked its head in there. Yes, we can grieve anything we lose, even if that loss is a major blessing. I grieved after I quit drinking, even though the stuff was killing me. Grief is our way of processing a loss – even if that loss is opening the way for us to soar.

Once I processed all those emotions – which basically meant sitting through them and FEELING them – I was cleared out and ready to move on. Ready to set my intention for 2023 and beyond.

Ready to make new magic. Ready to live a life I absolutely love.

We all deserve love, laughter, happiness and freedom. You just need to make up your mind you want it, be open to receiving it, and then take the right steps to achieve it.

✱·····LESSONS LEARNEd······℮

Once again, God was doing for me what I could not do for myself. Even though the job was burning me out, I wasn't going to leave it because of the steady money. Here was my push in a new direction.

Life is full of ups and downs and sideways twists. It's up to you if you get bent out of shape or learn to let go, let God, and look for the sunshine instead of the rain.

Freedom

As a teenage runaway on the streets of New York City, I was sure I had found freedom. After all, Janis Joplin said so:

"Freedom's just another word for nothing left to lose."

But just as my pets, pizza preferences and hair color has changed over the years, so has my idea of freedom.

Freedom now means not being held captive by that thing called alcohol. Not being stuck in old habits or ways of thinking that no longer serve me. Not surrounding myself with people or attitudes that only bring me down.

Freedom means having a choice in how I react to any given situation on any given day. This especially includes the episodes of hell on earth that are going to crop up as long as we're alive.

You can think of each episode of hell as a ball of clay being thrown at you. There are several ways you can deal with it.

You can stand there and let it hit you in the face, cry "I'm such a victim," and then go hide in the closet.

You can duck and not deal with it, letting the clay balls splat to the areas around you. That may seem like the easiest route – until, years down the road, you can no longer move because you're mired in a heap of built-up splattered clay.

You can grab the clay ball and try to throw it back, not realizing there's a boomerang inside it.

You can catch the clay ball and examine it, consciously determining how you're going to shape this hellish clay ball into something positive that you can use to move forward with more strength than ever before.

Certainly, the last option is the absolutely best. But it doesn't always happen immediately. Sometimes you might need to be hit in the face a few times, hide in the closet for a span, throw yourself a pity party or two, let several hell episodes build up, and then get angry and kick something (like a garden gnome).

Once you're in enough pain and thoroughly done with the suffering, you'll then have the motivation to shape the clay into something helpful, beautiful and worthwhile.

With enough practice, you may find you're shaping the clay into beauty more quickly than you used to. Then faster and faster still. Pretty soon, there's no such thing as a bad day. You grab that clay and shape it into something beautiful before it even has a chance to be anything else.

This may not happen immediately. Or even always. But if you're laughing and hugging more often than you're swearing and kicking garden gnomes, you're definitely on the right path.

And the right path is one that makes you feel good by consistently fueling your body, mind and soul with all that brings you joy.

....Lessons Learned.....

It's amazing how many things can hold us captive without us even realizing it. Alcohol was an obvious one for me, but I had no idea I was also being held back by resentment, old habits and fear.

Breaking free of everything that's holding you back is the most amazing way to experience a life beyond your wildest dreams – and you may even get a few goats, to boot.

Part 4
Making Magic in Your Own Life

Live in the magic.
It's much more fun
than living in the street.

-Ryn Gargulinski, 2021

High-Vibe Living

Have you ever seen those really happy dogs? You know the ones. They're not just wagging their tail – they're wagging their whole body.

I was having a day like that.

I don't remember what the weather was like outside, but my insides were bursting with sunshine. Every cell in my body was prancing with glee. Everything was aligned, just as it was meant to be. I was happy, floaty – a soaring eagle riding the waves of euphoria.

"This is amazing," I recall telling a pal. "But I can't feel like this every day."

"Why not?" she asked.

Ummm…uh…I don't know. Because I have to be boring and serious to make money? Because there's only so much joy to go around and I was already using up my fair share at the moment? Because it was my turn to empty the dishwasher?

As I was mentally reviewing my arguments as to why I wasn't "allowed" to feel like a soaring eagle every single day, the word "allowed" hit me square between the eyes.

A hidden chamber of my brain suddenly sprung open, ushering in the possibility that maybe, just maybe, I could be that soaring eagle every day. The only thing standing in the way was me. I wasn't "allowing" myself to have a great day every day.

It was high time to get out of this trap so I could be a full-time soaring eagle.

Why not, indeed!

That's what high-vibe living is all about.

Introduction to High-Vibrational Living

Everything is made up of energy, including ourselves. Energy is constantly vibrating.

- Things can vibrate at a low frequency, which is dense and heavy.
- Things can vibrate at a high frequency which is light and airy.

The vibrational scale, also known as a state of being scale, gives you an overview of 19 different vibrational scales here on earth.

- The higher the number, the lower you're vibrating.
- The lower the number, the higher you're vibrating.

Different emotional states of being are associated with each level. Check out the scale to see what I mean.

Meet the Vibrational Scale

High-Vibrational Zone

1. Enlightenment, Peace, Bliss, Euphoria
2. Joy, Gratitude, Appreciation
3. Passion, Love, Freedom, Wealth
4. Forgiveness, Compassion, Acceptance
5. Optimism, Willingness, Enthusiasm, Hope
6. Positive Expectation, Belief, Trust
7. Contentment, Courage

Low-Vibrational Zone

8. Pessimism, Boredom
9. Frustration, Irritation, Impatience
10. Overwhelm, Confusion
11. Doubt, Skepticism, Procrastination
12. Pride, Scorn, Contempt
13. Anger, Hate, Revenge
14. Desire, Craving, Discouragement
15. Fear, Anxiety, Worry
16. Grief, Regret
17. Apathy, Despair, Hopelessness, Judgmentalism
18. Guilt, Blame, Resentment, Depression
19. Shame, Unworthiness, Addiction

Note that addiction is at the very bottom of the scale. That means everything from pessimism to unworthiness was weighing down on my soul at the end of my drinking days. No wonder I was so miserable!

Illustration of the Vibrational Scale

I also did an illustration of vibrational scale which is harder to follow but a shade more artistic. Here you can note that FEAR ended up as a giant word smack dab in the middle, which I did not intend or plan. That just goes to show how big fear can be.

Not only are we vibrating at a certain frequency at any given moment, but we'll automatically attract more of whatever is vibrating at the same frequency we are. Basic law of attraction.

That means an active state of addiction is automatically attracting things like shame, unworthiness, resentment, depression, despair, hopelessness and all those other goodies near the bottom of the scale.

If you're flying high like that soaring eagle, you're automatically attracting things like peace, bliss, enlightenment, euphoria, gratitude and joy.

If you ask me, I'd rather have the joy.

A good rule of thumb is to try to maintain a vibrational frequency that's in the 1 to 7 zone. Once you hit level 8, you're snaking into boredom territory.

Since energy is in constant motion, there's no such thing as standing still. If you sit around in boredom for too long without taking any type of action to rise above it, you're destined to start moving down the scale.

Things will pull you down easier than you can pull them up. That's just the way it is.

We humans are programmed to look for and remember the negative. That habit stems from long-ago survival mechanisms. Humans would have to be on constant alert to look for danger, like things that might eat us.

Although we no longer have to worry about being eaten by a saber-tooth tiger, we haven't lost our penchant for seeking out the negative. Having lunch with someone who complains about everyone and everything gives you a good glimpse of that.

If you sit around too long in a bored state, you risk becoming one of those constant complainers. Negative thoughts may start creeping your way, sending an open invitation for even more negative thoughts, emotions and happenings in your life.

Continue to do nothing about it, and you may eventually end up at the bottom of the scale, slamming beer in an abandoned building in downtown Detroit with a mummified dead cat at your feet.

Well, you may not have to go that far down – but you get the idea.

That's why I make it my daily mission to do things that keep the vibrations high and the goodness flowing.

High-Vibe vs. Low-Vibe Habits

Daily habits are a solid start for raising your vibration. They also help maintain a high vibration once you achieve it.

You can spot-check your vibrational frequency at any time throughout the day. If you find yourself in a low-vibe zone, do something to get out of it.

Like what? Here come a few examples of activities that can help change your vibrational frequency.

High-Vibe Habit	**Low-Vibe Habit**
Waking up and saying a prayer	Waking up and drinking a beer
Making a daily gratitude list	Keeping an ongoing resentment list
Meditating	Ruminating
Processing and releasing emotions as quickly as possible	Stuffing emotions as far down as possible

High-Vibe Habit	Low-Vibe Habit
Listening to high-vibe music that makes you want to dance and play	Listening to low-vibe music that makes you want to punch someone

Make a list of your own habits to see which lift you up and which bring you down. Then try to swap out the low-vibe habits for new high-vibe ones.

Going Deeper

Changing habits is good, but it's still only scraping the surface. There may still be deeper, darker things embedded in your subconscious or clogged up in your past that are working to bring you down – sometimes without you even realizing it.

I certainly had a few (hundred) of them. They often surfaced as free-floating anxiety, where I'd go through each day haunted by an underlying sense of dread. I couldn't put my finger on exactly what was making me feel that way – but that dread went away once I began gutting out the hidden junk that had been collecting deep inside me.

And boy, was there a lot of junk. During one healing session with one of my spiritual teachers, she had a vision of pulling out big, long clumps of stuff – like long, thick strands of hair from a drain.

The more she kept pulling, the more stuff kept coming. She pulled and pulled and pulled some more until eventually it was all cleared out.

Whew.

It felt like there was way more stuff than I could have accumulated in a single lifetime, or even a single century.

The theory of reincarnation says our souls are reborn on earth again and again until we learn what we're supposed to learn to reach full enlightenment.

Things from our past lives that were never properly dealt with can continue to stick with us in our new lives.

I know in my current life I'm the packrat type that can have a hard time letting go of things. But who knew this applied to past baggage from a slew of lives I've already lived?

In any event, you may find great relief by digging deep and gutting out all the garbage.

It's also the first part of a process I like to call PSS.

The PSS process has three parts:

- Purge
- Stabilize
- Soar

Purge

Purging involves getting rid of things you no longer want. This can include everything from the too-small sundress you're keeping because it was a gift to the resentment against Susan O'Shanty because she gave you a drawing she made back in first grade but then took it back to give to Hildie Myerson.

Yes, I had hung on to that resentment for decades, not even realizing it was there. But it was there all right, interfering with my ability to trust and make new friends. It was also contributing to my low self-esteem.

None of this stuff is going to go away unless you actively do something about it.

Past resentments, fear, trauma, guilt, grief and other unprocessed gunk can end up jammed somewhere deep inside, festering, rotting, growing. Just ask that spiritual teacher who cleared all those strands of past baggage from my energy field.

Left unattended, these things can actually kill you. My dad is a prime example. I'm convinced his unprocessed emotions and other baggage was what was eating him from the inside out.

And it's not just the physical body that gets a big hit. Festering emotions can weigh you down on the spiritual, mental and emotional levels.

Purging out the junk gets rid of the old to make room for the new.

Stabilize

Stabilization is when you're in a balanced state. The old gunk is gone. You have yet to accumulate any new gunk. Your goal here is to keep it that way.

We're always going to have new challenges, obstacles, thoughts and emotions that may throw us for a loop. But if we meet those things head-on instead of stuffing them inside, they are less likely to leave us with residual baggage.

Here's also where you want to get rid of old habits, beliefs and stories that keep the door open for new garbage to come in.

One of the easier ways to get rid of an old detrimental habit is to replace it with a new beneficial habit. Instead of simply trying to stop playing the Scrabble game app on your phone for three hours a day, come up with another way to fill that time that's more meaningful – like playing with your dogs.

Before you know it, you're reaching for the dog leash instead of your phone.

Soar

Soaring means doing what you can to keep your vibrational frequency as high as possible at any given moment. Yes, we are going to dip into lower states of being as things come up. It's OK to visit anger, sadness, grief and other low-vibe emotions.

But you don't want to end up living there.

This is where you want to incorporate new habits, techniques and ways of thinking. You may also want to edit the stories you tell yourself. You want to make an effort to say and do things that bring you up instead of pull you down.

One tip I grabbed onto in early sobriety was sticking little positive affirmations all over my apartment. By my bed. On the fridge. On the bathroom mirror.

Even if I didn't believe all those things at first, I was told to keep repeating them as frequently as possible.

I remember telling my therapist at the time that all this positive thinking stuff in recovery was just like brainwashing. Repeating the same stuff over and over: I am worthy. I am beautiful. I deserve to be happy. Blah blah blah.

"It's just like brainwashing myself into the positive," I told her.

"What's wrong with that," she answered. "You had been brainwashing yourself into the negative for years."

Yeah, she was good.

The 12 Steps for Everyone

Instead of running around like a headless chicken trying to find a way to purge, stabilize and soar in every situation you encounter, you can get the PSS process done in one fell swoop with a magical thing called the 12 steps.

Originally introduced in the Big Book of Alcoholics Anonymous back in the 1930s, the 12 steps of AA have helped saved millions of lives by helping people to stop drinking and start living.

But the steps themselves are not just for alcoholics. They can be adapted to work for anyone, anywhere. That's because the steps do much more than teach you how to put down a drink.

They teach you how to live happy, joyous and free. I know. The "happy, joyous and free" promise can sound like some kind of marketing gimmick for Mount Airy Lodge.

In my first year of sobriety, I remember hearing that "happy, joyous and free" thing all the time. My response? "Happy, joyous and free my ass."

But guess what? Fast forward 23+ years and I actually AM happy, joyous free – at least most of the time. It didn't take a full two decades to get there, either. I started reaping the benefits of the steps as soon as I began honestly working them.

The steps have been adapted to help people with addictions that range from narcotics to gambling, overeating to smoking.

Addictions aren't the only thing they can help. My parents went to a 12-step support group after I ran away to New York City. It helped them realize they were powerless over my actions and how to let go and let God handle it.

My mom shared the moment she did exactly that. She had envisioned placing me in the palm of God's hand, saying it's all up to him, not her.

She told me it was one of the most difficult things she ever had to do, to relinquish all perceived control she had over how my life would turn out, but she knew it was the only way she could move forward.

She didn't know if I would ever be in her life again.

Once she was fully able to let go, I'm guessing He went to work right away. Based on the situations I put myself in and the rate I was drinking, I should have been dead at least a dozen times over.

"But instead, God brought you back to me," Mom said.

Our relationship has also been repaired. We actually enjoy hanging out together, especially when we go shopping. Heck, we took a road trip to the Grand Canyon together. She even let me talk her into staying at a haunted Flagstaff, Arizona, hotel.

We used to clash every time we simply looked at each other. Now I seek out her advice and her company. Even more shocking, she's sought out mine! I love her as both a mother and a friend.

12 Step Workbook

The steps are some powerful stuff. That's why I created the "12 Steps for Everyone" workbook designed for people not in recovery. It's a way anyone can benefit from the magic the steps deliver.

The steps provide the ultimate game plan to purge, stabilize and soar (PSS).

Coaching clients I worked with years ago still send me thank you notes for introducing them to the steps. They are amazed at how much calmer, happier and more peaceful they feel after weaving the steps into their lives.

To give you a glimpse of how you can use the steps in your own life, here's the way I adapted them in my workbook:

1. Stop banging your head against the wall.
2. Escape the craziness.
3. Get out of your own way.
4. Dig up resentments and fears.
5. Deflate the power of resentments and fears.
6. Root out detrimental habits.
7. Ask God to remove those detrimental habits.
8. Get ready for the great amends.
9. Launch the great amends.
10. Do your daily dusting.
11. Check in daily with your God.
12. Keep the momentum going.

Just be forewarned. The steps aren't for sissies. They ask you to go deep and be honest about what you find. I wanted nothing to do with them the first time I read them.

"How long can I wait before I do the steps?" I recall asking one guy at a meeting in my early recovery days.

"How long do you want to stay miserable?" he answered.

I've since been through the steps multiple times and can even pull one out of the hat to apply to any specific problem at hand. The results just keep getting better.

The Secret to Change

Change is possible, no matter how old you are or how long you've been engaged with habits, actions and ways of thinking that bring you down. But that change is only going to come if you're willing.

- Willing to embrace the unknown.
- Willing let to let go of what no longer serves you.
- Willing to do the work that makes that change happen.
- Willing to expect and accept good things.

You don't have to change everything all at once, or even one thing all at once. You can gradually shift into it. In fact, change typically follows a three-part process of its own:

- Awareness
- Acceptance
- Change

You can't change something you don't like unless you're aware – and accept – that thing exists.

Drinking is a great example of this one. I couldn't get sober until I admitted and accepted that my drinking was out of control and totally ruining my life.

Complaining is another good example. A chronic complainer is never going to stop complaining unless they realize and accept that they are constantly harping about the negative.

Here comes one more example, this one connected to self-esteem. I was not able to break out of the stagnant income zone I had been in for 10 years until I realized and accepted that I kept reinforcing my unworthiness with the stories I was constantly telling myself.

Once I changed the "unworthy" story to one of being totally worthy and deserving, my income began to – and continues to – increase. I wonder if you can get an extra tax write-off for high self-esteem?

What Next?

Just like there are dozens of different ways to change a lightbulb or make sassafras stew, there's no single right or wrong way to make high-vibe living a way of life. I'm sharing a way of thinking about it and acting on it that has worked for me.

Play around with the different ideas. Read other suggestions. I've included a list of the top books that helped change my life, along with resources you can check out at RynGargulinski.com.

Give things a try. The most important thing is to have an open mind – which leads to an open heart. And an open heart is how the magic starts in the first place.

Here's to creating your own magical life!

NOTE Above illustration is my sigil for my ongoing intention of making life even more magical still.

Books + Resources

Top books that enhanced my life:

Alcoholics Anonymous – Big Book
Alcoholics Anonymous

The Artist's Way
Julia Cameron

The Big Leap: Conquer Your Hidden Fear and Take Life to the Next Level
Gay Hendricks

Financial Alchemy: Twelve Months of Magic and Manifestation (Volume 1)
Morgana Rae

The Four Agreements: A Practical Guide to Personal Freedom (A Toltec Wisdom Book)
Don Miguel Ruiz

The Game of Life and How to Play It
Florence Scovel Shinn

Good Grief
Granger E. Westberg

The I Am Discourses, Volume 3 Saint Germain Series
Saint Germain, Guy W. Ballard

Where the Sidewalk Ends
Shel Silverstein

Resources for more learning and growing:
More details at RynGargulinski.com

- Reiki workshops, classes and sessions
- Kits, courses and course subscriptions
- Reiki meditation recordings
- Coaching and consulting for individuals, coaches and businesses
- Rynski motivational workshops and speaking gigs for your business, group or event

About the Author

I write quirky books. Create semi-creepy art. Spend way too much money on dog toys and crystals. Laugh so loud it makes people turn and stare. And I've never been happier in my life.

I didn't get drunk, get stalked, get homeless and then get sober and spiritual just to sit on my butt and play the Scrabble app (although I do that on weekends).

I'm here to help other people fall in love with and rejoice in who they really are. To break out of their self-made cocoons. To discover and live in their purpose.

This life is mine and I'm claiming it. How long before you claim yours, too?

RynGargulinski.com

More Books by Rynski

The 12 Steps for Everyone: An adaptation of the steps for folks not in recovery
Little Book of Big Jerks: Fast, fun illustrated guide for dealing with difficult people
Fun with Crystals: Workbook to create a delightful crystal connection

The Rynski Doggie Dictionary: Illustrated dog terms, expressions and proverbs
The Septic Bucket List: 22 Things NOT to do before you die
World's Best Bullet Journal: Raise your vibration, create success

Rats Incredible: An illustrated dictionary of rats
Bony Yoga: Illustrated yoga guide with skeletons depicting the poses
The Boy Who Had Moldy Cheese Pizza Under His Bed: A horrible fable with a tragic end

Made in the USA
Las Vegas, NV
20 March 2023

69395635R00167